W9-DER-608

CHRISTIANITY IN THE
EASTERN CONFLICTS

Other Books by the Author

JESUS CHRIST AND THE WORLD'S RELIGIONS
A FAITH FOR THE WORLD
THE FAITHS OF MANKIND

CHRISTIANITY IN THE EASTERN CONFLICTS

A Study of Christianity, Nationalism and Communism in Asia

BY

WILLIAM PATON

Secretary of the International Missionary Council
Editor of the *International Review of Missions*
Formerly Missionary Secretary of the Student Christian Movement
and Secretary of the National Christian Council of India

GEN. THEO. SEMINARY
LIBRARY
NEW YORK

WILLETT, CLARK & COMPANY

CHICAGO   NEW YORK

1937

275 T
P 274
104119

Copyright 1937 by
WILLETT, CLARK & COMPANY

Printed and Bound in the U. S. A. by
KINGSPORT PRESS, INC., KINGSPORT, TENNESSEE

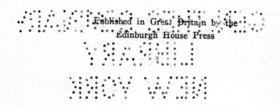

Published in Great Britain by the
Edinburgh House Press

AUTHOR'S PREFACE

I HAVE explained in the introductory chapter how this book came to be written. Things change so rapidly nowadays in the " unchanging East " that some part of what I have said about current events may well be out of date by the time the book is published. Even so, I hope that the diagnosis of underlying forces may stand a longer scrutiny.

If I could enumerate them, I should wish to thank the men and women of many nations with whom, during the crowded months of the journey out of which this book arises, I had conversation about their work and the conditions under which it was carried on. Any freshness of treatment and reality of insight is due to these priceless contacts with people in the forefront of the battle.

I have to thank my colleagues, Miss Underhill and Miss Standley, for help in the revision of the manuscript and in the collection of material. To Miss Wilson of the United Council for Missionary Education, and to certain members of the council, I am indebted for much advice and for invaluable help in seeing the book through the press. My principal indebtedness I have acknowledged elsewhere.

W. P.

St. Albans, *October,* 1936.

Copyright 1937 by
WILLETT, CLARK & COMPANY

Printed and Bound in the U. S. A. by
KINGSPORT PRESS, INC., KINGSPORT, TENNESSEE

Published in Great Britain by the
Edinburgh House Press

CONTENTS

INTRODUCTION

THIS book is based chiefly upon the experiences of a journey which it was my good fortune and privilege to undertake during the autumn, winter and spring of 1935–6. Traveling from England through America and Canada, during seven months I visited Japan, Korea, Manchuria, China, the Straits Settlements, Java, India, Egypt and Palestine. The principal object with which this journey was undertaken was to discuss with representative Christians of the indigenous churches and with missionaries in the different countries the plans that had been outlined for holding in the Far East, in the autumn of 1938, a world meeting of the International Missionary Council, in succession to those held in 1910 at Edinburgh and in 1928 at Jerusalem. These plans were made in outline at the meeting of the committee of the council in Northfield, Massachusetts, and I left the meeting to go directly to Japan, there to begin an intensely interesting process of testing, in innumerable discussions, whether the themes which the council had chosen as the subject matter of its proposed world meeting were in fact the most important.

It was suggested to me that out of the journals which I wrote on the journey and sent to a number of friends I should try to make a book. But books, if they ever come alive at all, insist on shaping their own life, and what I have finally put together is more than a record of impressions. I have divided it into two parts. The first part is an attempt to state what seemed to me to be, in the light of the study possible in the course of my journey joined to such previous knowledge as I had, the most important facts in the life of the four great regions of Japan, China, India and the Near East, looked at from the point of view of the growing Christian church. I am very well aware that in trying to cover so much ground I have laid myself open to the charge of being dogmatic and superficial. I can only say that I had the opportunity of meeting and talking with an extraordinarily wide variety of people, and that I have tried to be objective and not to fit the facts to the theories which come so readily to the mind in such a world of change as this.

The second part of the book is an attempt to discuss, a little more thoroughly than can be done in the course of a factual description, certain of the outstanding questions by which the Christian church is faced as it addresses itself to the task of witnessing in these lands to the Christian gospel. The first question that rises in the mind, filled with the great events and movements that are transforming the peoples before our eyes, is of the gospel itself. Is the missionary enterprise, as it has been suggested, the spiritual efflorescence of Victorian bourgeois prosperity, doomed to pass away as that prosperity has passed away, a notable intercourse of peoples and races but not more, at bottom, than the fruit of a social movement? Is it rooted in the eternal? Is there a word of God that speaks to men of our age as to those of other ages, and that is supremely relevant in the great conflict of loyalties that is going on around us?

Next, I believe, comes the characteristic question of our time, namely, the relation of the Christian church, in which the word is preached and believed and lived, to the community and to the state. The work that is being done in preparation for the world conference on church, community and state at Oxford this year is most relevant to the missionary enterprise. My earlier chapters show, I trust, that this is a problem of supreme practical importance and of great urgency. It is one which is now occupying many of the best minds of Christendom, but I do not think that its importance for the rising churches of the East has been sufficiently noticed.

I have commented upon two other main issues, the life and witness of the church, and the relation of the church to the changing social and economic order. A living church will manifest its life principally in the two activities of worship and witness; witness, if it is truly Christian, will not be only in word but in deed, and the environment within which the church's life is lived not only changes so that new methods of witness are needed, but challenges the word and the life that are the heart of the church by flat denial. Here are many and difficult questions—I can only hope to have stated them and shown their gravity.

The central thought which recurs always to my mind as I think over all that I saw, and over much that has happened since, is of the living church in a world of incalculable change. It is terribly easy to simplify things (especially for the purpose of public speech) so that all reality escapes, and so vast a canvas cannot be covered by a few lines. Yet I think that it is true to say that the church is faced today with both menace and hope. On one side we can see the gathering of forces which are likely to set greater and greater difficulties in the path of the church, and may even threaten its very life. On the other there is the great uprising of the spirit of evangelism and the turning of minds and hearts to the Christian message, if not yet with belief, at least with arrested attention. Both things are true ; perhaps they are parts of the same fact.

In such a world the Christian church is to find and do, as God gives it the power, the will of God. I hope that it does not sound arrogant in spirit if I say that the meeting of the International Missionary Council in Hangchow in 1938, the preparations which will precede it and the labor that will follow it, are planned in the hope and prayer that they may be used by the church in this task of finding, of *hearing*, the word that God is speaking in the concrete situations of our time. The meeting is to comprise about four hundred delegates from all parts of the world, and it is intended that more than half shall themselves be indigenous members of the churches of Asia, Africa, and Latin America. The decision so to compose the membership represents another step in a process that goes back through the meetings held at Edinburgh and at Jerusalem. At the Edinburgh meeting in 1910 (the effects of which upon the whole ecumenical Christian movement were so great) only a handful out of a total of some twelve hundred delegates were not of American or European race. At Jerusalem in 1928, out of about two hundred and fifty delegates over fifty were members of the " younger " churches (the phrase was coined in the meeting, and, although not satisfactory, it at least avoids describing some churches as " native " when all are native, or describing the larger part of the earth as the " mission field ").

At Hangchow the meeting will be essentially a meeting of the " younger " churches, joined by representatives of the church life and missionary administration of the West. The central theme is to be the church, the universal historic Christian fellowship, especially as it is found and is being built up among the Eastern and African peoples. Within this central theme there will be further studied the faith by which the church lives, the witness of the church in evangelism, the life and worship of the church, the relation of the church to its environment in the social, economic and political order, and the need for a greater coherence and unity of action on the part of the Christian forces. The meeting will be merely the focus of a period of combined prayer, work and thought extending over some years. The object of the whole endeavor is that the church,[1] or

[1] The word " church " is used, unashamedly and of intent, in different senses. Sometimes it means a local congregation or community, sometimes what we call a " denomination," but chiefly it is used to indicate that wide and somewhat vague and yet intensely real fact,

such part of it as is willing to work in unison in spite of diversity of life and order, shall be aided by thorough study and by common consultation in the supreme task of learning the will of God for our time.

I do not think that we should be afraid to say even so bold a thing as this, if we say it with full recognition of the fact that it is not in our own effort or ability to command success, and that it is God who speaks and we who listen.

The present book has come to be for me an attempt to state some of the matters which the meeting in the Far East will have to face. But I hope that any who read this statement will not be deterred by it, for the book is not about meetings and conferences but about the world and God.

the company of Christian people in the unity which they possess in spite of their division. In the main I have had to omit the Roman Catholic Church from consideration because the hope of common consultation and action is still debarred by the policy of that body. I have *never* used the word " church " to denote the clergy or ministry—a deplorable though all too common habit.

PART I

THE EAST TODAY

I

JAPAN

" JAPAN is the most important single fact in the
modern world." The man who said this to me
over a dinner table in Calcutta, two or three months
after I had left Japan, was scarcely exaggerating.
Japan *is*, at the very least, as important in her inherent power, in her inevitable relation to other nations, and in the underlying spirit and doctrine of
her national life, as any other people today.

I shall always be glad that my first visit to Japan
was made across the Pacific from Canada and not by
way of China and Korea ; for I do not think that
anyone whose first acquaintance with Japan was
through her imperial expansion could fail to be in
some degree turned against her, and to that extent
rendered unable to appreciate her native spirit.[1]
Here is one of the most remarkable peoples in the
world. They believe that they are uniquely qualified to provide the meeting place of the cultures of
East and West. They look back to an ancient and
continuous national history, whose origins are
wrapped in mists. They rejoice in institutions, the
imperial house above all, as venerable as the country's own history. They know themselves to be filled
with a restless energy and resource. They look at
what other nations have done in the world when the

[1] Probably the same is true of us British—I do not know.

17

chance came to them, and they believe, with complete national unanimity, that this day is their day and that they have a work to do.

Just because there must be in what follows much that is radically critical of the Japanese national spirit in its relation to other nations I am anxious to put first this impression which Japan so powerfully forces upon the mind. Take the union of cultures. There can be no such thing except on a basis of equality, from which every trace of uneasy patronage or subservience has been removed. You have that in Japan. The externals of city life are of the West ; indeed the trains, the restaurants, the great department stores speak of America rather than of Europe. The universities are based upon a virtually universal literacy, and they breathe freely in the atmosphere of all the world's scholarship. While the Christian colleges look mainly to America, the government universities look rather to Germany.

In economic organization the Japanese have learnt all that the West has to teach. I do not know whether there was a time in Japan when Japanese culture was looked down upon by those who were learning the new, but if ever there was it has passed. Along with the eager acceptance of what it believes the West has to give there is a proud insistence upon the Japanese spirit. Buddhism is alive and advancing, and Shinto—much more typical of Japan than Buddhism—by its national cultus molds the very life of the people and the policy of its rulers. Even if it is held that the culture of Japan is less profound and less original than that of China, the conditions for an equal meeting of East and West are present. No European would be tempted to patronize a

Japanese in Japan ; and equally no Japanese feels himself bound either to slavish admiration of the West or to the petulant overcriticism of it which is the mark of the inferior.

It is rash for a stranger to speak about the culture of another nation, especially upon the basis of a short visit. But there are things in the private life of the people that speak eloquently of a delicate and beautiful understanding of the art of living, a love of old ways that is not the result of sloth but of a strong sense of continuity. I felt this deeply when I was admitted to the ceremonial tea-drinking in a Christian Japanese home. It is a beautiful ceremony. The tea is prepared and served by the wife or daughter, with a slow, deliberate, restful ceremoniousness which I found wholly delightful. Or again, the old castles and the lovely old paintings speak of an ancient and delicate culture which is not forgotten in the modern Japan of the skyscraper and department store but lies deep down in the national consciousness.

The bookshops give a glimpse of one side of the Japanese determination to master the secrets of the modern world. In Tokyo are some of the finest bookshops in the world. Even in Osaka—a great cotton city rather like Manchester with but few foreigners living in it—I found bookshops offering well known books in several European languages for both first and secondhand sale. I had not expected to find that Hebrew grammars command a sale in Tokyo, but I was seriously assured that professors in the imperial university were learning both Greek and Hebrew in order to be able to get at the Bible for themselves.

In the industrial field the same sense of unity and power is conveyed. I need not exhume figures about Japanese exports from blue books to illustrate what everybody knows, namely, the extraordinary rise in Japanese exports. Undeniably the wave of Japanese goods that has flooded every market in the East and far beyond it has presented very great difficulties to the other industrial nations. But it should be realized that this export trade is essential if Japan is to feed her people. Extensive emigration is prohibited to her, and in any case it does not appear that the Japanese are, like the Chinese, a people that can " swarm," going in masses to other lands, there to bring up their children.[2] The Japanese seem to have set their faces in another direction : they will feed their people by exchanging manufactured goods for food and raw materials. They must succeed in this or perish, and the working classes work with something of the patriotic *élan* which all Japan puts into the national task. When I read something like this in a report of the International Labor Office I feared that Geneva had waxed sentimental—but it is true.

Behind this unity and this impressive demonstration of national purpose, however, lurk other factors that are ominous. There are elements of grave division among the people. Economically the condition of the villages is different from that of the towns. The primary producer all over the world has been getting very little for his crops since the great depression began, and Japan is no exception. Taxation in Japan is high, as it must be when we remember not only the colossal expenditure, largely met by loans,

[2] The colonies of Japanese in Brazil and the Philippines hardly disprove this observation.

on armaments and military expeditions, but what must have been demanded by the rebuilding after the earthquake of 1923. The villages look to the army, which is essentially of the countryside in both officers and men, to bring them the prosperity they lack, though it is hard to see how, for instance, the Manchurian adventure can do other than increase the competition with which the farmer must contend.

If city and village are in some measure opposed economically, within the urban mass populations are also the latent forces of division that exist in every industrialized society. One reason for the timing of the Manchurian invasion may have been the desire to distract attention from the growing problem of the socially conscious proletariat of the cities, and to drown the voices of socialism and communism in a flood of patriotic emotion. This at least was the result; and it is plain to any observer of the social movement in Japan, and even of social service and ameliorative agencies, that all effort of that kind is at present carried on with much difficulty and under constant suspicion.

The conditions of life of the Japanese industrial workers are superior to those of the workers of China and India. It was put to me by a foreign worker in this field that if one took the figure ten to indicate the level of life of the factory operative in one of the great Western industrial countries and the figure one to indicate the level in India or China, the figure for Japan would be somewhere about five. I mention this with some diffidence, for I have no claim to speak out of personal investigation, but it is perhaps fair to state it. A labor leader with whom I had conversation in Osaka spoke freely of the discontent among the working men, and asserted that the prosperity of the country was not reflected among the masses or indeed anywhere except among the great capitalists. And yet I was conscious during our conversation that he was saying much less than I had expected to hear, and far less than later on I heard from social workers in Shanghai.

But whatever be the comparisons that it is fair to make between the conditions of factory workers in Japan and in other Eastern countries, there can be no doubt that the fear of subversive action on the part of an organized working class is very much present among the rulers of Japan. Communism is both ruthlessly suppressed and greatly feared. It has, as in other countries, its attractions for the younger intelligentsia, and every effort is made to prevent the circulation (or, as the customs examination so profusely shows, the introduction into the country) of communist literature or anything that might be held to contain " dangerous thoughts." Thirty thousand people were arrested for complicity in communism between 1930 and 1935. It is curious to reflect that in every country some people in important positions hold that ideas of this kind can be kept out by physical means. Communism is not an empty theory ; it offers an explanation of present facts and a prophecy of their alteration. Those who, like the present writer, differ totally from the communist view cannot deny that the social facts need altering even more than they need explaining. Japan is industrial as no other nation of the East has ever been. About half her people live directly upon machine industry. She is also a highly capitalized country, with great concentration of wealth in a few hands. Japan will have to face the same social struggle as all other nations that have embarked upon industrialization.

It is not surprising, therefore, to find that there has arisen, particularly among the younger officers of the army, a school of thought very closely resembling fascism. The army, as I have already said, is rooted in the rural life of Japan, and there is some sincerity in the plea that it stands in the name of patriotism against the financiers and capitalists and the liberal type of politician, who are supposed to be in the pay of big business. This plea has been somewhat harder to sustain since certain leading figures in the army and in the navy were involved in financial scandals ; but it is probably true that the type of social order in which the younger army type of mind believes is what is called the corporative state.[3] One hears rumors of a demand for sequestration of the property of one or another immensely wealthy family to help to meet army charges. Undoubtedly this type of propaganda made it easier for the army to carry through the Manchurian invasion and the subsequent advance into China ; for it appears to put the country before private gain.

I turn now to that feature of Japanese life and thought which, from the point of view of the Christian church, seems to be most dangerous, namely, the complex of ideas centered in the doctrine of the divinity of the emperor. I shall return to the use that the army is making of this, for the doctrine itself is of far wider range. The emperor has a place in the national life probably unique in the world. The

---

[3] I.e., authoritarian government through functional groups rather than by representative democracy.

dynasty is held to be descended from Amaterasu, the sun-goddess. It is certainly continuous in line since before the Christian era. (If the Olympic games go to Japan in the year 1940 they will coincide with the celebration of the twenty-six hundredth anniversary of the foundation of the Japanese imperial house.) The emperor is not to be thought of merely as the supreme executive, or as the organ of the state. This theory, usually referred to as the "emperor-organ theory," and associated with the name of Dr. Minobe, has been officially proscribed. The accepted view is that in the emperor, by reason of his divine quality, all power inheres, and he can bestow it on whom he will. The whole people in a sense shares in this divine quality, and the essence of the Japanese spirit is the wholehearted acceptance of this special quality and worth of the Japanese nation.

The doctrine is accompanied and supported by the rite of emperor worship. About this rite much has been written and much controversy has gathered. There are certain shrines set apart for the observance of "state Shinto," a cultus to be distinguished from the many and varied sects of denominational Shinto. In these state shrines the officiants are frequently retired officials, generals or admirals; and while the government, through its bureau of religions, exercises a general supervision over all Shinto worship, as over other worship, state Shinto is directly carried on by it.

There is a steadily increasing pressure, especially on the schools, to take part in the rites of state Shinto. Sometimes no more is required than a visit to the shrine and a bow in the unadorned, austere holy place. Sometimes the pupils are compelled to be present at rites in the shrine, where prayers are made to the divine ancestors of the nation. The army instructor, placed on the staff of every Japanese school by the army, is naturally a person of great importance, and it is from him that this pressure proceeds. The official defense is that these ceremonies are not religious but patriotic ; that the constitution of Japan declares the freedom of religion ; that compulsion to follow any one religion is, therefore, unthinkable ; and that all must cordially join in those ceremonies which are necessary for the unity and well-being of the nation. It is important, in this connection, to remember that in Japan there are practically no primary schools except those conducted by the state, and that in these schools the full doctrine of the emperor mythology is taught.

A word much used in the discussions on these subjects, for which no English translation seems to be quite exact, is the word " *kokutai,*" which means something like " national substance." " Community " and " *Gemeinschaft* " are near it, but the philosophy of *kokutai* has to be understood in its own light. I take the following from a newspaper article by a Japanese writer :

Any thought or movement, however strongly it is supported by the public . . . will suddenly be stamped as being rebellious and lose its support when once anything contradicting *kokutai* is found in it. . . . *Kokutai* is a social idea including such meanings as national substance, national principles, and national form, and is not a mere political idea. . . . Ours is a nation that began with the " transfer of the country " carried out by the sun-goddess and was completed by the " stating of

the country " accomplished by the Emperor Jimmu
—a sacred land reigned over by august emperors,
coeval with heaven and earth, whose imperial
throne is occupied by a single dynasty. . . . Its
constitution is different from those of other countries. . . . The empire was founded by making,
according to divine command, natural laws and
justice crystallize into state and life. . . . Who
founded Nippon ? It all goes back to the sun-
goddess and the other gods . . . who created or
ruled this country. These numberless gods became the standard of the mind of the people, and
from this was born the idea that Nippon is a sacred
land. This idea has been inherited from god to
god, from the ancestral gods to the nation founding
gods, and then to their successors, the gods in human form (the emperors) , and has led the people
to " worship the gods," " comprehend the gods'
will," " abide by the gods' principles," and " arrive
at the gods' virtue." This is how this sacred land
of ours has grown up, and this way of thinking has
become the very nature of " the people of the sacred land."

Why did the gods found the country of Nippon ?
Because they wanted a place where they could
realize their will. The place that was chosen first
is this land of ours, and the people are in duty
bound to be obedient and to adjust themselves to
their rule unconditionally, thus making the will of
the gods the standard of everything. . . . Thus it
is evident that Nippon was established in a way
not to be found in any other country : the creator
gods ; and " Michi " the will of the gods ; and the
Emperors, the descendants of the gods who inherit
the " Michi " and rule ; and the subjects who work
united with the emperors in one body ; and the
territory, the material element that fulfills the

work of the gods—these five have crystallized into one. . . . All of this has led to Nippon's national activity and social progress, its politics, learning, military power, industry and all other things, expanding for the purpose of carrying out the gods' will. . . . The study of Nippon *kokutai* is the duty of us Nipponese, and the decree of the emperors Jimmu and Meiji is that we shall concentrate to set a good example of a righteous country before the world.

Let us assume that the above passage represents a fairly extreme form of the doctrine, though I doubt whether it does. It will at least indicate the sort of national philosophy with which we have to do in Japan. It will be expounded differently by people of different outlooks. Those who cling to liberal ideas will try to interpret it as merely a spirit of patriotism, and will accept the official apologia that the prescribed rites are not " religious." Those who look to a military expansion on the basis of a fascist type of social organization will find this religious philosophy admirably adapted to their need. It appears that the officer group who were behind the murders of February 1936 (in which Takahashi, one of the most courageous and far-sighted men in Japan, met his death) were exponents of this idea. They held a mystical view of the imperial mission of Japan, recognized that the money for expansion could not be found under a liberal capitalist order without an intolerable increase of taxation which would be ruinous to the farmers, and therefore, with a truly revolutionary spirit exactly analogous to the left wing movements of other countries, slew the liberal finance minister and demanded a radical reorganization of the resources of the state.   The London *Times* correspondent remarked of this movement, known as the Showa restoration movement :

> It is, fundamentally, the Japanese response to the modern revolutionary impulse.   The " divine discontent " which impels it along is aroused, here as everywhere else, by the contrast between the wealth of society and the poverty of individuals. It is not communism, it is not the New Deal, but it shares their faith that miracles can be wrought if only the state controls the economic machinery. In other nations the clamor of the masses for a fuller life inspires the demand for a greater diffusion of wealth.   In Japan, where conditions and background are different, it comes as a need for greater government revenues to promote the security and welfare of the nation by military means.[4]

I know that the importance which I am here ascribing to the emperor-worship issue is not accepted by many, perhaps most, of the leading Christians and foreign missionaries in Japan.   It is pointed out that Christians are allowed to make it clear to all concerned that they accept these rites in the sense in which government ordains them, namely, as acts of patriotic veneration and nothing more.   It is also urged, and this with much practical wisdom, that the constructive policy for Christians to follow is to avoid direct collision with the state and to try to put into the minds of those whom they may influence a truer notion of God and of worship, so that false and crude notions may die away.

Even so, conflict lies ahead ; and it seems to me,

[4] The London *Times*, July 14, 1936.

influenced as one must be (and I think rightly so) by some knowledge of tendencies elsewhere in the world, that we are beholding in Japan the clearest instance in modern times of the regimentation of the state, in all its parts, round the idea of its own absolute sacredness. Already there are signs of interference with the intellectual liberty and integrity of the universities. Just as in Germany the Nordic obsession has produced the most amazing ethnological theories from otherwise eminent scholars, so in Japan we find arguments solemnly adduced to show that Japanese recorded history is twenty thousand years old. A committee was established some years ago to try to reach an understanding on the question of shrine worship, but no agreement could be found, and the committee has now abandoned its task. In 1930 an informal conference [5] took place between a leading government official and a group of Christians in which some searching questions were put in the desire to discover whether the government, in stating that the rites were non-religious, based its statement upon a thorough examination of what took place in the shrines. This is the all-important question, and the simple truth is that it has been answered evasively in every official statement. None of the doubts, clearly and admirably expressed in that conference, seem to have been removed. On the contrary, there are now examples of the persecution of Christians as such. Inquirers and converts are sometimes exhorted to keep away from this internationalist and un-Japanese religion. Sometimes the influence of the military instructor, even in Christian schools, is such that no Christian work is

[5] See *Japan Christian Quarterly*, July, 1930.

possible. I have heard of a teacher's being arrested because, in reply to a child's question, he stated that Jesus was greater than the emperor. A Christian in Kobe was imprisoned and severely dealt with because he denied that the sun-goddess was divine and refused to worship the emperor.

The feeling that behind all this is a policy of state expansion, based upon the religious absoluteness of the state, is confirmed when one finds, as I did in Korea, that shrine worship is being pressed there with even greater vigor than in Japan proper, and that it is enforced also in Formosa and in the mandated islands of the Pacific. For Christians in Korea a crucial situation immediately arises, for they have not the patriotic feeling for the emperor and the tutelary heroes that Japanese have, and they regard the demand that they should engage in shrine worship as tantamount to a demand that they should return to idolatry. In Korea earnest efforts have been made to reach a form of observance possible to Christian consciences and yet acceptable to the state —e.g. in which it might be made plain that the spirits of the heroes, believed to be present in the worship, are not so present—but the use of any such form has always been refused. The state demands its worship on its own terms.

I found myself driven to the conclusion that when a government, while urging that the required observances are patriotic and not religious, so steadily adheres to its demands, refusing alternative versions of its rites that would be free from religious misunderstanding, it really means that what it demands is *more important than religion*. Or, to put it another way, it uses the word " religion " to denote sectarian and private cults ; for its own observance it reserves that absoluteness and universality of range which belong to true religion.

While it is necessary to face the logical meaning of this movement, I must not write as though there were no other tendencies but these in Japan. The election held last February resulted in a considerable measure of success for the more radical of the two great parties, and incidentally brought into the House an increased number of Christians. There is much concern over the growth of the military budget and the expanding plans of the militarists. Though little unprejudiced news of China is available to the ordinary Japanese reader, and there is a surprising amount of conventional talk about the " chaos " prevailing in that country, wiser heads can see that in the struggle between the two powers, were it carried through to the end, the fate not of China alone but of Japan also would be involved. Men will say to you in private, " I do not know of a single person of education and judgment who really approves of what has been done by the army leaders in these recent years." I have been told that when the extreme nationalist party sought to organize the students of the Imperial University of Tokyo they could secure only some eighty members in a university of about five thousand. This has to be put against the unquestioned fact that the army is popular with the mass of the people.

Nothing in this connection is more important than the signs that the educational authorities are now of a mind to modify the extremer nationalist tendency so far as the life and teaching of the schools is concerned. (It must, of course, always be remembered that the *army* authorities can act apart from other authority, and this, I believe, applies to the army instructors whose pressure has been felt in the matter of shrine worship.)   There is concern even among moderate conservatives, as well as among liberals (I do not, of course, use these words in a technical party sense) about the narrowness of military ideals in education, and about the danger of the imposition by the military mind of a mechanical type of education such as to prevent any development of private judgment in the pupil.   During 1935, the minister of education sent an instruction to all schools to abstain from any restrictions upon, or interference with, authorized religious and moral instruction.   The intention was to encourage anything that would make for individual character and independence of judgment. The ministry sent to colleges, universities and higher schools a deputation consisting of a Shintoist, a Buddhist and a Christian, charged with the duty of encouraging religious activity in these institutions.   I am told that later the ministry ordered all primary schools to introduce more teaching based upon the lives of heroes of moral and cultural advance, and to lessen the tendency to concentrate attention upon the lives of military heroes.   Mr. Takata, the head of the bureau of religions, attended as a visitor the all-Japan Christian conference held in November, 1935, to explain on behalf of the minister of education a new religious bill shortly to be introduced into the parliament.   Among the provisions mentioned was one to secure proper educational and moral qualifications for religious workers.

I hope that whether or not this estimate of the situation which faces Christianity in Japan is felt to

be just, at least it has been made clear how complex
and difficult that situation is.

Let us now consider the Christian forces in Japan.
There are about four hundred thousand Christians
—Orthodox, Evangelical, Anglican and Roman
Catholic. Exact numbers are difficult to state, for
the familiar reason that different bodies employ different statistical bases ; but the number of " church
members " returned by the Anglican and Evangelical churches in 1934 was almost two hundred
thousand. The Orthodox metropolitan, Sergius,
puts his community's number at forty thousand,
of whom, he added to me with characteristic candor,
he would count perhaps twenty-two thousand as the
effective number. The most striking fact about the
extension of Christianity in Japan is its slight hold
upon the villages and its relatively large influence
among the educated and " middle class " people.
There are relatively few places of worship in the village areas, and one of the hoped-for results of the
visit paid to the United States by Dr. Toyohiko
Kagawa in 1936 was the creation of a fund for building a large number of rural churches. On the other
hand, one is constantly surprised by the position of
influence that Christians possess in the leadership of
the country. At the time of the coronation of the
present emperor, three of the five presidents of the
imperial universities of Japan were Christians.

It is especially in the sphere of education that the
Christians are influential, though they have an honorable record also in the different forms of social service and not least in the education of the social
conscience. Both in regard to the narcotic evil and
in combating the traffic in vice they have been con-

spicuous, though the power of commercialized vice in Japan has long been great and it takes courage to oppose publicly and vigorously a traffic which is not afraid to use the violence of hired ruffians to defend itself against attack.

Japanese Christian leaders are well aware of the fact that until now there has been little mass evangelistic work done by the church in Japan and that a great number of the Christians do not know how to approach the villages, with which they have had but little contact.   There are historical reasons for this, of which all that need be said here is that the gospel came to Japan as *teaching,* and that the most immediate opening that offered was among the students, who had been aroused by their contact with Western knowledge and made alert to the challenge of new truth.   But, as one Japanese friend wistfully said to me, " The people in the villages are satisfied ; they *have* a religion."

The " Kingdom of God " movement which began in 1929 under the leadership of Dr. Kagawa had as one of its objectives to double the Christian membership in Japan.   But it would be misleading to lay much emphasis on this numerical goal, for in the movement there were two main elements always present :   a genuine zeal for conversion, shown not merely in an efficient organization but in the great volume of prayer stirred up among the Christians of Japan ; and an effort, conceived in Kagawa's own spirit, to unite evangelism with social practice in the form of the cooperative movement.   This is not the place to offer any estimate of the kingdom of God movement—there is some question both about the firmness with which the double objective was maintained and about the degree to which the movement was integrated with the life of the churches. In November, 1935, at the all-Japan Christian conference, a new united evangelistic movement was begun. In this it is hoped that the churches will join together more fully and (in the right sense) more officially than before, and that a persistent attempt will be made to find a way to the mind and heart of the villagers. There are plans for the formation of a school for training in rural evangelism linked with other forms of rural service, a line of work which, as we shall see later, other countries are beginning to pursue.

Japanese Christians like others throughout the East are impatient of the divisions which have accompanied the coming of the gospel, and there is a strong movement in which laymen are conspicuous for achieving a large measure of unity. One of the reasons for this movement is undoubtedly the sense that the Christians are all too few and that they must act together if their witness is to be effective. Another aspect of this consciousness that Christianity in Japan needs to be equipped to deal with its task is to be found in the considerable interest taken in modern theological movements. Professor Karl Barth has many followers in Japan, and it is said that certain Buddhists claim to have discerned his teachings in the Buddhist books! There is a steady stream of translations of theological works into Japanese—I noticed Bultmann's *Jesus*, a leading book of the "form criticism" school, in the list—but as I have already said, the touch of Japanese thinkers with the outside world is nowadays more by direct use of foreign books than by resort to translation.

I was greatly impressed by the genuine concern felt by representative Japanese Christians for the Christian welfare of the outlying parts of the Japanese empire and the countries under Japanese influence. The Overseas Evangelistic Association is not concerned only, though it is in part, with ministering to Japanese abroad; it is deeply concerned also with the evangelization of the peoples of Formosa, Manchuria and Jehol, and the mandated territories of the South Seas. While I was in Mukden, during my brief stay in Manchuria, I met a young Japanese and his wife who had been sent from Japan as the first missionaries of this association to the people of Jehol, and there was no mistaking their missionary spirit. Here is one of the signs that show how the secular ambitions of Japan affect her religious life. (Incidentally I noticed that a good deal was being said in Japan about the extension of Buddhism in other countries and particularly in the West.) It is not an exaggeration to say that on a small scale the same thing is happening within Japanese Christianity that happened within British Christianity at the birth of the modern missionary movement. It is merely foolish to write this off as " spiritual imperialism." In each case there has been a realization—through colonization or discovery or extension of national influence—of the existence of other lands. It has borne fruit among Christians in a sense of evangelistic responsibility.

In no way, however, do the Japanese Christians so clearly show their sense of being linked with the rest of the world in responsibility for giving and receiving as in their attitude toward foreign missionary activity within Japan. I cannot exaggerate the earnestness with which many of the most representative Christians urged in my hearing their sense of the importance of the continuance for many years yet of the missionary contribution, not merely in money but in men and women. This is the more remarkable in that Japanese Christians are in unquestioned control of the activities of the Japanese churches. The missionary has passed almost completely from the position of leadership which he still holds to a large extent in India, and even to some extent in China. Whether the Japanese leaders, absorbed in the tasks of the churches, have given sufficient thought to the place of the missionary under modern conditions in Japan, I am not so sure. But when it is suggested that the missionary is no longer needed and should be withdrawn, there is genuine consternation. It was put to me by some of the best men I met in some such words as these : " We know that our Christianity is weak in numbers, very young— practically all of it arisen since 1860, and therefore lacking in maturity and experience of its own. We know also that we have to present the gospel and witness to it before our ancient people, with its long continuous traditions and its keen sense of national continuity. We need to be backed up by the rest of world Christianity, and to be helped to feel ourselves a part of a world fellowship." It was for this reason that the Japanese National Christian Council so strongly urged that the next meeting of the International Missionary Council should be held in Japan.

Here, then, are some powerful arguments for the view which forced itself upon me, that the future of Christianity in Japan is a matter of great importance to the whole Christian world. There is, first, the consideration that springs from the strength and importance of Japan herself. Whatever we may think of some things that the Japanese government has done and is doing, it is not to be denied that a good deal of the history of the world during the coming generation is being planned in Tokyo. The Japanese are a people of great resource; the very fact that the nation believes itself to be misunderstood by other countries, and to be reproved for doing only what others have done, makes it more self-assertive. Japanese Christians believe that as members of the Japanese body they must try to bear a Christian witness, and that upon their success in so doing much may depend for the world.

Second, there are the difficulties and dangers which beset the Japanese churches as they face their task. If what everyone says is true—that there is a national revival in Japanese religion—it is not a revival that helps the Christian faith. It flows easily along Shinto channels—that hardly needs saying. It flows easily, too, along Buddhist channels; for Buddhism, though alive in Japan and performing a teaching office, can easily accept the syncretistic union with Shinto which the nationalist revival implicitly suggests. But nothing can ever obscure the fact that there is about Christianity something exclusive.

Moreover, as I have tried to show, there is at issue for Christians something more serious than a measure of unpopularity in a time of national exhilaration, or an inability to take the same advantage of a vague national religiosity that others can. It may be that the elements in Japanese life and thought that desire to make the state religiously absolute will confirm their already formidable hold upon the country. At present, though there are exceptions, the general view of Japanese Christians is that the " non-religious " explanation of the rites on the part of the government may be taken as sincere, and the required observances accepted in that sense. I think that, apart from a genuine affection for the emperor and a wish not to weaken the emperor institution, they take this attitude in the belief that the groups in national leadership who think more or less with them will come out victorious and the militarist theology fall out of fashion. On any reading, the situation is one full of peril ; it might easily become one of acute and terrible danger. For there is no doubt that the militarist section is definitely anti-Christian—and very properly so, for it is utterly impossible to accommodate any kind of Christianity to the beliefs which I have tried earlier in this chapter to sketch.

Yet even these hopes and dangers do not quite reach to the depth of the appeal which I feel that Japan makes to our common Christianity. I can best convey it by telling the story that was told me at the Poole School, conducted by the C.M.S. for girls in Osaka. There was a great typhoon in Osaka two years ago, followed by a tidal wave, and in the devastation that engulfed the city the building of the school partly collapsed. Some seventeen girls were killed. They were caught beneath the fallen beams, unable to move and terribly crushed, and while they were waiting in the faint hope of rescue one among them, herself a non-Christian, asked that prayer be made and a hymn sung. A Christian girl prayed and all those who were able joined in the words of "Abide with Me"; and so singing and praying they died before they could be rescued. The newspapers of Osaka heard of the story. "What is this religion," they asked, "that teaches Japanese girls to die like Japanese soldiers?" I spoke with the principal of the school, a Japanese Christian who had himself been rescued when at the point of death. He told me, in words which I will try to repeat, of his own spiritual experience in that time of agony : "I saw a brightness and wished to advance toward it, but when I tried to do so I could not, for I was held back by my sins. So I came back to life, and now I know that God has spared my life so that I might be more fully given to his service."

The nearness of the Japanese to great physical disaster, their tradition of the chivalry of the *samurai*, their own spirit of utter surrender to the emperor— these facts all make them a people to whom religion appeals most of all in the heroic. Here is the secret of the success of that great Japanese Christian, Kagawa. He is consumed with the desire to be identified with the sufferings of Jesus Christ upon the cross.

The supreme service that the church as a whole can render to Japan and to Japanese Christians is to help them into the deepest understanding of Christianity, in thought, action and worship, for only a discipleship both passionate and profound will move this people.

II

CHINA

I SAID that I was glad to have entered Japan for the first time from the Pacific and not through her dominions on the mainland. I came to China, however, through Manchuria, and I do not think that the terrible picture there unfolded gives one a wrong introduction to the China of today. The shadow of Japanese advance lies dark over the future as Chinese who love their country look into it. Perhaps what has happened in Manchuria may be repeated even more widely in China. In any case it would be utterly unrealistic to write of modern China without recognizing the master fact of Japanese policy and all that flows from it.

For Japan, the issue of Manchuria, or Manchukuo, is settled. Even those Japanese who opposed or doubted seem now to be of one mind with the rest. I need not elaborate their case—Japan fought Russia for Manchuria and was kept out by Europe ; she has not only given her blood for the land but has great material interests there ; the Manchus wanted autonomy, and though force was used it was only used in the same way that the Allies used force to establish the Czecho-Slovak state ; China is in a state of chaos ; Manchuria is Japan's " life line " ; and in any case, what superior righteousness have the Western states shown that they may take a high line over Japan's necessary action in Manchukuo?

On the essential point of fact, namely, whether the people really wanted a government of their own, separate from China, neutral opinion appears to be emphatic that they did not. It is a fruitless plea, anyway, for what they have got is not in any sense a Manchurian or local government but the military government of a Japanese dominion. It is more useful to ask what Japan means to do with it. There is much talk about a Japan-Korea-Manchuria economic bloc. I am afraid that I must anticipate my narrative and add that usually a fourth member is joined to those three—North China. It would be quite impossible in this little book to deal at all fully with the highly complicated problem of Japan's economic position in relation to her oversea adventures, for it is a tangled web into which come considerations of Japan's food supply, her possession or lack of raw materials, her dread of communism, her need at all costs to sell her manufactured goods, her relations with Russia, and of the place of Russia in the European balance. But it is reasonably certain that no one in Japan really thinks that great masses of Japanese are going to live in Manchuria. They have sent only half a million Japanese to Korea where the climate is kindlier. It was remarked to me, " There are three things Japanese want and cannot get in Manchuria—baths, schools and newspapers."

Let us say, then, that for a combination of strategic and economic reasons Japan (and this must be taken to mean not merely a military party but practically everybody who is vocal) is convinced that it is necessary for Manchuria to be integrated with Japan. The tragedy of the situation is, in part at least, that so little of the beneficence which civilian Japanese honestly believe must follow in the train of the " emperor way " is to be found in Manchukuo. It is a purely military regime ; the so-called Kwantung army of Japan is all-powerful, and Manchukuo is not the first state in which the establishment of a military authority over a sullenly resentful people has attracted a low type of man to the posts of power.

Not long before I reached Mukden there had been a considerable number of arrests, mainly of leading Christians, pastors and doctors, the effect of which had been virtually to immobilize the Manchurian church. The facts of this matter were withheld from public comment by the missions, out of the well grounded fear that publicity would rebound upon the heads of the unfortunate Manchurian Christians. The main outline of the story has, however, appeared in the London *Times* and elsewhere, and it can do no harm here to say that some sixty persons were arrested without charge made in any court, held for questioning, in some cases tortured in extremely modern ways, and only released (in most cases) after weeks spent in jail under the severest conditions. I do not think it necessary to hold that this action was actuated by specifically anti-Christian motives. The type of person who rules Manchukuo is, all over the world, highly credulous ; there had been an acknowledged failure to suppress banditry and anti-Japanese guerrilla warfare ; there must, it seemed, be some center where educated people, in touch with the

outer world and especially with China, were inspiring these movements ; what more likely than that
the Christians, who possessed almost the only educated leadership among Manchurian Chinese, were
at the bottom of it ?   A society—most innocent in
its simple philanthropy—was discovered, possessing
a name reminiscent of certain communist organizations, and it was obvious to the governing mind that
here was communist anti-Japanese agitation.

Even were this all, it would bode ill for the future
of Christianity in Manchuria.   Those who are behind the Manchurian policy are not the liberal
civilians of Tokyo, but the fanatical exponents of a
military mystical faith.   What they want is to eradi-
cate the Chinese-ness of the Manchurian population
and to weld them into a spiritual and cultural unity
with the people of Japan.   Hence—and surely I am
not wrong in finding this highly significant ?—the attempt to institute in schools in Manchuria the compulsory worship of Confucius.   It would not be
appropriate to institute the specifically Japanese
cults, for Manchukuo is, in name, a free and auton-
omous state, entirely independent of Japan.   But
Confucius is a Chinese sage whom all Chinese honor.
Let the same principle of the state religion, that yet
is not religion, be applied here.   I heard of a most
illuminating speech made to a group of school teachers by a leading Japanese official, the burden of
which was that they must strive to get the recognition of the state as the first obligation to be acknowledged—then, he handsomely admitted, " religion
would not stray from the path."

How can there fail to be conflict between such a

policy, ruthlessly carried out, and any church that is true to its message and duty?

I have suggested that these considerations may not unfairly be applied not only to Manchuria but to the wider field of China, south of the wall. It was my fortune to be in Peiping just before what was humorously called " autonomy " was launched, and to be in Nanking during those anxious days when, through the firmness of the Nanking authorities, the negotiations about the North had been transferred from the Japanese generals to the diplomats and the Japanese ambassador was closeted with General Chiang Kai-shek. I was able to gain at least some insight into the problem as the Chinese saw it, and I make no pretense that my sympathies were not deeply engaged by the Chinese in their time of racking anxiety.

I do not think that there is any reasonable doubt that the present rulers of Japan desire to establish a hegemony over the whole of China (I am not thinking of Tibet, Sinkiang and other outlying parts for long subject to nothing but a titular Chinese sovereignty). They do not think in terms of conquest and annexation, but of the exercise of a compulsion over the whole of Chinese political and economic life, of which the ground will be the existence of a reserve of force far greater than anything that China can command. All the polite phrases about desiring " sincerity " in China, about a common front against communism, about the repression of anti-Japanese activity, mean in effect that the life of China is to be directed toward Japan, that it is to be turned away from the West, and that in all the greater matters of national life and the major concerns of statesmanship China shall obey the behest of Japan. There will then be, as is reiterated times without number, peace in eastern Asia.

It is important that those who care for the freedom of China recognize the elements of weakness in the Chinese situation. Professor Tawney has pointed out that there has never been in China any great politically educative system such as that which Rome imposed on Europe, leaving behind it, long after Rome had perished, the sense of the *res publica,* of the majesty of the common law. China is, in consequence, a race and a civilization rather than a state ; she has not had the tradition of the great state, and she has, for geographical reasons among others, never had the clash with the outer world that made the European states. Now she has come into a world of militant nationalism ; in economics as well as in certain other departments of life she has had to leap from the fourteenth century into the twentieth, and she is not a state in the sense in which Japan is a state. Traditions of social morality that worked not too badly in a vast community whose general stability was untroubled from without for centuries at a time, the exaltation of the claims of the family, the apotheosis of the literary scholar—these and many other ancient traits of the national character need now to be modified if China is to be able to assert her national right in time.

I think that a great many Japanese have honestly come to the conviction that China cannot organize herself in the modern world, and that if Japan does not take on the task the predatory West will. On the other hand, I find an increasing number of foreign observers who believe that China only needs to be given a fair chance, and who are greatly impressed by the moral as well as the technical quality of the men who labor in the harness of the Nanking government.

It is easy to twit that government with its lack of effective control over the whole of China. It is remarkable that its writ runs as far as it does. There is no other Chinese government conceivable ; its work in improving communications, by road and air, has been notable ; it has greatly reduced in the last two years the communist enclaves in certain parts of the south and west ; it has faced the rural needs with vision and resolution ; its dealing with the Canton revolt of 1936 was, if difficult for the outsider to comprehend, undeniably effective.

To avoid accusations of anti-Japanese activity it has had the courage to submit its own people, their newspapers and books, to a virtual censorship in the interests of Japan. It has never been confronted with specific demands from Japan which it could accept or reject, and know what it had done. Even the three demands of Mr. Hirota when Japanese foreign minister—recognition of Manchukuo, a common front with Japan against communism, sincere abolition of all anti-Japanese activity—are, all but the first, vague. Already the organized smuggling in the north has decreased to a ruinous extent the revenues of the Chinese government, while the illicit traffic in narcotic drugs, in which Manchukuo plays a large part, has attracted the alarmed attention of the world. I was told by a good authority that there are two hundred thousand drug addicts in the city of Tientsin alone, and eight hundred thousand in the Tientsin area.

North China—comprising the five provinces north of the Yellow river—contains over half of China's coal reserves, the same proportion of her iron reserves if Manchuria is not counted, nearly half of her supplies of wheat and other grains, nearly half of her railways and a fifth of her population.[1] To unite this area with Manchuria, Korea and Japan might be a strength economically to Japan—though it appears that, even there, a party exists that strongly prefers economic and trade expansion among the more thickly populated and prosperous southern regions—but it would be a ruinous blow to China, and no Chinese government can assent to it and survive. To press such a demand to the end would probably mean that everything left in China that could move and plan would unite with the Chinese communists, whose anti-Japanese feelings are not in doubt—an ironical outcome for Japanese policy.

But what can China do ? This is the question that is in every mouth. Ought we to fight ? Is it right to fight ? Even though we know that we are far inferior to Japan in military power, is it not better to fight than to yield to demands that we and all the world know to be unjust ?

Some minds are turning—I found this in Nanking —to a middle course which yet would not be merely a temporizing between resistance and submission. It might be possible for the Chinese government to try in the firmest possible way to reach an agreement, frankly yielding any points on which the special

[1] From E. M. Gull in the *Nineteenth Century*, August, 1936.

needs and position of Japan might entitle her to be
heard, provided they did not injure China, and making clear in the most public way the grounds on
which, in the interests of the country, they could go
no further. If this should prove fruitless, then let
China, while publicly refusing as unjust the demands
made upon her and avoiding war which, as things
are, could only bring upon her the most terrible
suffering, seek to organize every kind of moral resistance.

This course would be very difficult to follow, much
more difficult in the initial stages than a resort to
war. It would demand not only the highest moral
courage but a measure of unity in the country, or in
enough of the country to make it effective. It would
not be easy to hold together the vocal elements in
support of such a policy, for a large part of the student population, so much more influential than in
Western lands, is wholeheartedly for war. Further,
the enemies of China know how to stir up trouble
behind the lines, so that they may with a show of
reason demand to come in and restore order. Nevertheless, a resort to war would, it is certain, lead to
the most terrible suffering and disorganization
throughout the country and could not but end in the
disappearance of every type of free Chinese leadership ; while the alternative of submission would
immediately destroy the present government, which
would lose support on all hands.

Let us now, supposing that China is left in freedom to put her house in order, consider some of the
things that cry out to be done. China is an agricultural country, and the growth of industrialism, while
in certain regions a perceptible factor in economic

life, is still relatively small. It is indicative of the comparatively small place as yet taken by the " great industry " that four-fifths of the cotton cloth used in China is the product of the hand loom. The combination of evils under which the villager labors staggers the imagination. Debt, high rents, lack of communications, illiteracy are some of them. The sheer cheapness of human labor strikes the onlooker as symbolical of the conditions of life in the country districts. It has been estimated that 20 per cent of the population of China is occupied in transport. One would think that the conditions of life under which the ricksha men in the cities carry on their work would make it impossible for the firms to recruit any pullers, but it appears that the life is better than that from which they come.

When we find that the peasants pay, on the average, one-half of their crops in rent for the use of their land, it ceases to be a matter for surprise that there are " no-rent " movements. Here is Professor Tawney's description of the rural scene in much of China :

Over a large area of China the rural population suffers horribly through the insecurity of life and property. It is taxed by one ruffian who calls himself a general, by another, by a third, and, when it has bought them off, still owes taxes to the government ; in some places actually more than twenty years' taxation has been paid in advance. It is squeezed by dishonest officials. It must cut its crops at the point of the bayonet, and hand them over without payment to the local garrison, though it will starve without them. It is forced to grow opium in defiance of the law, because its military tyrants can squeeze heavier taxation from opium than from rice or wheat, and make money, in addition, out of the dens where it is smoked. It pays blackmail to the professional bandits in its neighborhood ; or it resists, and, a year later, when the bandits have assumed uniform, sees its villages burned to the ground.

Mr. Tawney goes on :

What is called the communist question is in reality, in most parts of the country, either a land question or a question of banditry provoked by lack of employment. It appears to be true, nevertheless, that in China, as elsewhere, an elemental revolt against intolerable injustices has been organized and given a doctrinal edge by political missionaries, and that certain regions . . . with an abnormally high percentage of tenants and acute agrarian discontent form enclaves of revolution, where such government as exists is conducted by communists.[2]

It is an indication of the spirit of the present government in Nanking that after driving out the communists from Kiangsi it embarked upon a vigorous policy of rural reconstruction. In this it has been notably aided by a group of Christians who have formed the Kiangsi Christian Rural Service Union, with headquarters at Lichwan. In this province a coherent attempt is being made to tackle the related problems of rural credit, land tenure, marketing, education, road-making and all the rest. It is interesting to find the dean of the theological

[2] R. H. Tawney, *Land and Labor in China*, pp. 73, 74.

school of Yenching University leading this Lichwan experiment, and not less interesting to be told that after experiencing some opposition from local officials the government made one of the union workers district administrator.

Mass education is another huge task at which Chinese, both unofficially and with government initiative, are working vigorously. The best known name in this field—and deservedly so—is that of Dr. Y. C. James Yen of the mass education movement. I tracked Dr. Yen down until I found him addressing a Rotary club luncheon on a boat in the Canton river, and there heard him say—and he adhered to it under cross-examination—that it was possible for China, even with her present economic resources and organization, *entirely to remove illiteracy*. It is, by the way, both interesting and important to find that Dr. Yen is now engaged not only in the conquest of illiteracy, taken by itself, but in a comprehensive scheme for rural uplift in which education plays a vital part.

Such men enable us to look at the terrific Chinese problem with hope, for they have hope and they know more about the difficulties than we can. I think of another Chinese, whom I had known when he was a student in Britain, now in charge of the ricksha board of the Shanghai municipal council. As he told me of the reforms that had been initiated against the most unscrupulous opposition of powerful vested interests—he smiled as he said that they had offered a reward for his murder—I could not but feel it desperately wrong that such men should not be left free to do their best for their country. They may not be many, and it is fair to say that too many of the scholar class have been prepared to profit by the Chinese tradition of respect for the literati without doing anything in return, but they are an earnest of what may be.

While the major problem of China's reconstruction lies in the rural areas, it should not be forgotten that in a country with a teeming population, pressing ruthlessly on the land, there must be a growth in industry if there is to be any raising of the level of life. This, of course, depends even more upon the continuance of peace and satisfactory political arrangements than does the rural development, for a measure of foreign participation is inevitable. But it need not be assumed that this means for China a great increase of the big factory, crowded into a few areas. To some ways in which these problems are being faced I shall return again.[3]

What of religion in China? I think that there is an unmistakable turning of people to religion, and it seems to be due, as one would expect, to the tremendous difficulties by which the nation is confronted. One hears, as in Japan, of a great development in new sects, many of them blended of Taoist and Buddhist as well as of animistic ideas. The most important movement, however, is the lay revival in Buddhism. It does not seem to have affected the Western-educated classes to any great extent, though there are important exceptions and some Christians of education have embraced Buddhism. But it is a movement of middle and upper class Chinese, men and women, apart largely from the monks and nuns

[3] See Chap. VIII.

of the monasteries, formed into brotherhoods and sisterhoods and trying to learn the wisdom of the Buddhist books and to find there consolation and guidance for the perplexities of the present day. Their leaders are in some cases reforming monks, such as the well known T'ai-hsu, and they have adopted many of the methods of Christian activity. T'ai-hsu considers that Christianity may perhaps be regarded as a special form of Mahayana Buddhism given to the Western races. But this friendliness is unusual, for the spreading of Christian ideas among a large number of intelligent Buddhists not only has caused them to examine more rigorously their own books but has led them to a vigorous opposition to Christianity as the only effective rival of Buddhism.

Dr. K. L. Reichelt, whose Christian mission to Buddhists at Kowloon is a wonderful example of great scholarship joined to evangelistic fervor, believes that this lay revival of Buddhism is the most important religious movement in China apart from the Christian church. He finds in it a certain number of Christians who have come to believe that Christianity is merely a pragmatic business, that churches are all " drives " and " campaigns," and that it offers no place to the man who wants deep and quiet meditation. Others testify to the same thing. Here are men—many of them middle aged ex-officials—who find in the Buddhist metaphysic and its teaching about desire and the abolition of the self the key to the woes of the world. At the same time there are Buddhist scholars in Dr. Reichelt's institute who are finding their way to the truth as it is in Jesus.

Among the student classes there seems to be general agreement that the choice lies between Christianity and some non-religious position. There is much evidence that the confident humanism so lately the mode has weakened in the present national plight, and that young men are not so sure as they were that " science and socialism will save the state "—a great slogan not so long ago. I listened with amazement to the story told to the executive committee of the National Christian Council of China by three Christian professors who had made a tour of a great many colleges and universities, holding in all of them evangelistic meetings. They found that the former hostility to Christianity had vanished ; there was plenty of criticism of what the students knew as Christianity, but also, and far more important than that, a keen desire to find whether in the gospel of Christ there might not be both a way of understanding life with all its pain and difficulty, and also a way of living. They found this spirit at least as much among the students in the government colleges as in those of the Christian institutions. They estimated that in the course of their campaign they had addressed or otherwise come into contact with one hundred and fifty thousand students and youths, and they summed up their impressions by saying, in Miss P. S. Tseng's words, " These youths are thirsting for a spiritual change and they are trying to find out whether Christianity can supply it." Miss Tseng defines the major conflicts with which young China is concerned in a series of antitheses : Materialism versus spiritual reality—China cries out for more and more science, but students are coming to feel that more than science is needed to save them and their

country from destruction.   State control versus individual rights—dictatorships are fashionable and
China needs a strong central government, but has not
personal freedom a sacred meaning ?   Ultra-national-
ism versus internationalism—China needs intense patriotism, but must one suspect and hate all nations
but one's own ?   War versus peace—China has always
honored peace, but war seems to be the only way out,
and yet Christ's teaching suggests another way.   Communism versus Christianity—much of the communistic ideal seems to be taken from Christianity, and
both aim at a world revolution, so that students wonder which has the future.[4]

There is another direction in which the breaking
out of the religious spirit is to be seen in China,
namely, the remarkable growth of a revivalist type
of preaching and fellowship in a considerable part of
the country.   Such movements as the Little Flock, or
the remarkable work of Dr. John Sung, are cases in
point.   Invariably these movements proceed upon
the foundation of a highly conservative theology and
view with suspicion all human learning.   They are
divisive in their impact upon the ordinary Christian
congregation.   Where a congregation has become imbued with their spirit there is an almost complete
breach between it and any group of Christian students in a college or school.   (I saw more than one
distressing case of this myself during my short stay.)
But the fact remains that, when all this has been said,
souls are being converted to God through these
means, and ardent life and power carry their own at-
tractive quality everywhere.   I cannot count the num-

[4] See *Chinese Recorder*, April, 1936.

ber of occasions on which Chinese pastors raised with me in conversation, or in semiformal conference, the question of the attitude they should take toward these movements. I could only say that where souls are converted to God there is a work of the Holy Spirit, and that it is for us who differ from the methods and from the setting of the message to examine ourselves to find in what ways we lack a truth and a power that others have.

Education presents important problems to Chinese Christianity. The proportion of the whole education provision in China which the Christian bodies supply is still considerable (there are 3500 students in 18 Christian colleges out of a total of 40,000 students in the whole of China, and 196 middle schools with 30,000 pupils out of a total of 1892 with 400,000 pupils). But this proportion has decreased rapidly in recent years as the resources of the state and of private Chinese generosity have been opened up, and it must decrease further. It is in quality, as has often been said, that the Christian contribution must be made, and this will involve a concentration and elimination for which missionaries and Christians in China are no more ready than those in other lands—which is to say, hardly at all ! But in addition there are special problems imposed by government regulations. Registration has now been accepted by many of the mission institutions. It carries with it obedience to the regulations concerning religious instruction. In primary schools no teaching of religion is permitted. In middle schools and colleges it may be offered as an elective subject—a system, of course, entirely different from the " conscience clause " of India. It would seem that if religious instruction is permissible at all it is obviously more important for the very young, but when I urged this upon an eminent (and friendly) official I was told that the government considered that religion should not be taught until students had reached an age at which they could fitly make up their minds on these matters.   The orthodoxy on this point—it is always uttered with the air that accompanies the promulgation of obvious truth —is perhaps in China to be traced to Mr. Bertrand Russell.   The policy would seem to entail, at least when applied to private schools which receive no aid from the state, a plain interference with civil liberty. However, people in China have their own ways of doing things, and I am bound to say that no educator with whom I spoke was in any doubt about the fact that through his school or college and in connection with it he had abundant opportunity for all the religious work he had it in him to do.   I should add that a good deal of evidence exists to show that there is genuine friendliness in official quarters to the Christian schools, and that they are welcomed.

One may here mention the "New Life" movement, with which General Chiang Kai-shek himself has been greatly concerned.   It is an attempt to instill into the people a certain modicum of ethical principle, in some ways harking back to the Confucian ideals of manners and social rectitude, and in the areas where special rural reconstruction is being carried out the New Life ideas are being pressed.   Some Christians hold that the movement ought to be warmly backed by the churches ; others feel that it is shallow ; some call it fascist—these are left-wing people who suspect

General Chiang and his government. I should doubt whether it is likely to be a considerable force, for the main reason that in a situation so grave as that in which China stands religion has to be tremendous or nothing.

There are two fundamental needs, I think, that must be met by Christianity in China. One is for depth in religion—depth that is both spiritual and intellectual. The other is for the spirit of community. One might put it otherwise and say theology and the church, but that might rouse angry passions. If it is true that among the many issues confronting the ardent and disillusioned youth of China is that between Christianity and communism ; if they have got away from the foolish crudity which would suggest that Christianity defends one social order and communism another, and have come to realize that each in its own way claims to give a *true* account of the meaning of life—then it is imperative that the Christian faith in its depth and fullness be taught to such minds. Again, if it is true that some who have been Christians have become Buddhists because they found in Christianity only a pragmatic address to life and in Buddhism a profounder dealing with the great questions that have always vexed the minds of men, what graver criticism could be made ? I was reminded, when this was said to me, of the remark made by a deeply devout Hindu after a long conversation with a group of Continental scholars at an international student gathering in India. " I never knew," he said, " that Christians had a cosmogony." There are, I dare say, more important things than cosmogonies, but it is not worthy of the Christian faith that thought-

ful souls should be able to conceive of it as merely a
practical scheme of living, apparently agnostic on the
ultimate questions. We are conscious enough in the
Western world of the need for a continual and radical
labor of thought on the message of the Christian religion ; we recognize how the categories of human
thought change, and we know how easy it is for Christian theology and apologetic to become a mere churn-
ing up of old controversies, learned and unprofitable.
In China (and throughout all the East) there is the
same onset of the modern world with its materialism
and its new love of authority, its myths before which
it bows down, its economic terror and its sense of defeat. But the ancient cultures are present in the
background, and in many minds the new secularism
is built upon a debris utterly different from the preconceptions of the Western mind. There is, therefore, a crying need for more theology and better
theology.

The church, as fact and idea alike, is little understood, it seems, by many Chinese. One meets eminent
Christians, of unimpeachable conviction and enthusiasm, who seem hardly to belong to any visible com-
munion, and do not quite see why they should, except
that it is usually done. I distrust all general apho-
risms (especially applied to nations or to women),
but I remember having been told that " the Chinese
understand the school, they do not understand the
church." On the one hand you have a certain number of church bodies of which their critics say that
they are concerned only with maintaining themselves,
and that they are valueless for the great causes to
which Christians in China ought to be giving them-

selves. On the other, you find men of great authority urging that what matters is not the church but the " Christian movement " in China, and that it is in the latter, not in the former, that living power is to be found. We shall come back later to this fundamental theme. I would say here only that the church, in its true meaning and according to the New Testament vision of it, seems to me to be fundamental to the whole Christian witness in China, and that it is most necessary that impatience with a multitudinous denominationalism, itself a travesty of the truth, should not be allowed to divert attention from what has been vital all down the ages to the Christian witness.

It is not hard, then, to see the hope and the peril of Christianity in China. With all the weaknesses that can be attributed to it—and most of them are the result of Western limitations—it is arresting the attention of those on whom the full tragedy of China most presses. It offers a gospel of which the center is One whom all men, be they haters or lovers of him, instinctively recognize to be alive in their own world. Suppose that China were to try in the face of Japan the method of united moral resistance, following on an earnest attempt to make honorable peace, that I mentioned earlier as occupying some of the best Chinese minds. It would be difficult to carry out for two reasons : it would demand great moral strength and willingness to stand to the end for what is right in principle ; and it would mean holding together the whole country, in the face of ancient rivalries and without the stimulus of a common warlike adventure. I would not claim absurd things for the Chinese

Christians, but I think that they have something to bring to a great nation at such a time of testing.

For these reasons there may be hard and perilous times before the Chinese churches. I suggested early in this chapter that it was not by accident that the Christians in Manchuria were the objects of the wrath of the state, for they could not but be a standing contradiction of the twin ideas of totalitarian state authority and an introverted nationalism. If these influences should, by one path or another, come to dominate China, it is to be feared that the church would again be the most obvious obstacle, just because it is in some measure integrated over all China, it is linked with all the world through its missionary connections, and it owns an exclusive allegiance to its Master which it cannot barter away without conscious apostasy.

I read recently a sermon by my friend Professor T. C. Chao of Yenching on "The Message of the Cross." His final word was this : "But what is the message for the church and for individual Christians when the issue is faced squarely ? It is very short. It can be summed up in the one single word 'martyrdom.'" I have found other hearts heavy with the same thought.

Nevertheless, I would rather end this chapter on another note. We can easily drift into thinking that because certain tendencies seem inevitable and men are getting ready to fight on one side or the other of the issues they have stated, there is a fundamental necessity in the matter. There is no such necessity. It is still folly, the result of the blindness and timidity and selfishness of men. The Christian way of peace and understanding is not a foolish quixotry offered to a world essentially alien to such thoughts ; it is the wisdom of God. There is therefore always a task of reconciliation. But this is utterly different from all mere dexterity in formula-finding or uneasy straddling between opposites. It is based upon the belief that the true interests of men in a world that God made are reconcilable, and it has behind it the knowledge of a supreme reconciliation wrought not by the act of man but by that of God.

There are many Christian people in the Far East today who recognize that upon those who believe in the divine principle of reconciliation there does lie a special burden in these days. It is a fact of the highest importance that in Japan and Korea, in Manchuria and China, there are Christians, men and women, some of whom have learned to know and trust and love one another across the barriers of nationality. There are also Western Christians in these Eastern lands who have friendships in more than one country which transcend the national lines of cleavage. It should be possible for some way to be devised whereby, in the humblest spirit and with no thought of anything but the service of the peoples, a spirit of realism in the discussion of difficulties and of reconciliation in the face of past antagonisms might be conveyed and interpreted. To some such service, not less valuable because it must be rendered in quietness and obscurity, some among the Christians of the Far East may be called, and in it they should be upheld by the prayers of the universal church.

III

INDIA

IT IS an instructive experience for one who has lived in India to return to it by way of the Far East. Light is thrown on many Indian problems by a glimpse of the very different conditions of Japan, China or Java—the last an entrancing country, of which within the scope of this book I can say nothing, though the study of a land where government and Christian effort alike are so largely in the hand of a single people, the Dutch, is full of suggestion. Memories of Japan, Korea and Manchuria make a Briton wonder how far he has been overcritical of government policies which he does not condemn when they come from his own people ; not that the British government propagates emperor worship, but a good deal of the Korean complaint against the Japanese is not unlike that of the Indians against the British. Or again, the roads, the railways, and the homogeneous, efficient administration of India suggest how much China has yet to accomplish in that regard, while also one cannot but recognize that independence stimulates public spirit as subjection can never do. A former Indian civil servant was quoted to me in Hong Kong as saying, "You may think this strange as coming from an Indian civilian, but the thing that impresses me on coming from China proper to Hong Kong is the lack of public spirit."

It is not easy to describe the temper of Indian public life in these days. I was conscious of a good deal of disillusionment and loss of spirit among a number of those with whom I talked. In the political sphere the five years that had passed since I had seen India had been packed with event. I had left on the very morrow of the agreement signed between Lord Irwin (now Lord Halifax) and Mr. Gandhi, and I well remember the sense of relief that was felt when the news came through. Since then had come the second and third Round Table conferences, the laying of the British government's proposals before Parliament in the form of the White Paper, the long discussions and the report of the Joint Parliamentary Committee, the Government of India Bill, the intense feelings aroused in Great Britain by the campaign of Mr. Churchill and his friends, and then the passing of the act. They had been very full years, viewed from the standpoint of British constitutional action. On the Indian side they had been not less full, and much more tragic. First there was the participation of the Indian National Congress in the Round Table sessions, but in the sole person of Mr. Gandhi, delegate plenipotentiary. Hope had risen in many quarters that on his return to India there might be a new attempt at constructive peace, but this hope died as war was declared between the government of India and the Congress (a contest for which a good many on each side seem to have been spoiling) and a period of vigorous repression ensued. There followed the smashing of civil disobedience; then came the rise of the " untouchables " issue into a foremost place in public life through the increasing identification of Mr. Gandhi with it ; then the growth of communal feeling ; a general disapproval of the new act, though not from uniform reasons, and now a widespread discussion of the problem whether there should be active cooperation with the new constitution or obstruction, office-acceptance or boycott.

To many people it seems that neither constitutional action nor the chosen way of Mr. Gandhi—non-violent non-cooperation—has brought anything worth having. The fruit of the former, they feel, is the new act, and I must in honesty say that I have met with virtually no Indian enthusiasm for it. Keen nationalists look at the undoubtedly powerful " safeguards " and laugh at the idea that there has been any real transfer of power. Socially progressive people fear that the large share of power given under the federation plan to the princes' nominees will limit the possibilities of the kind of progress they want. Liberals are nearly as bitter in denunciation as congressmen, for they feel that their cooperation has been flouted. It seems reasonably certain that there will be a large measure of cooperation with the new institutions, but it would be useless, in my judgment, to pretend that there is any enthusiasm.

Equally disappointing to its supporters have been the fruits of the revolutionary movement. I call it that, for I think that in essence the Congress today is out for a revolutionary change. It has for some years ceased to believe that much could come from negotiation with the British government ; and its leaders, with engaging frankness, explain that they do not expect the British, any more than others, to give up voluntarily the power they now possess, or to yield place for any cause except that they recognize a new power in the Indian people. Readers of that intensely interesting book, Pandit Jawaharlal Nehru's auto-biography,[1] will recall the sense of exhilaration with which the leaders of the civil disobedience movement entered on their campaign in 1930, and the high hopes reposed in the " non-violent " method. But the Congress has had to face the fact that the government had taken up the challenge, and that its vigorous campaign of repression had succeeded.

I put these things down because it seems to me very important that British people should recognize the existence of a great deal of bitterness in India. It is not at present focused in any movement, and it could be dissolved, I believe, by generous action. But it is there. One of the main effects of the campaign of opposition to the India bill waged in Great Britain has been that the British public has never listened to the Indian case. It has believed that it had to choose between a government measure characterized by great and perhaps rash generosity, and an opposition based upon motives of caution or of economic nationalism. That there was an Indian criticism, as strong as Mr. Churchill's though entirely opposite to it, was very little appreciated.

If Indians imbued with political enthusiasm come to be convinced that neither in constitutional action nor in the Gandhi technique of " non-violence " lies any hope of success, there is a danger that they may choose a third way, that of revolutionary violence. I do not think this likely, for terrorism is alien to the Indian temper, and the existing terrorist movement

[1] *Jawaharlal Nehru : An Autobiography* (Lane).

has been mainly a Bengal phenomenon and attributable to certain special influences. But we must recognize that there has come into being a strong left-wing political group within the Congress—led by no less a person than the president of the Congress, Jawaharlal Nehru—which has learnt something from the experience of the social revolution in the West and will undoubtedly try to use the instrument of social unrest as a political weapon. In fairness to them I must add that in doing so they believe that they are taking the only way that will benefit the very poor. To men of the stamp of Jawaharlal Nehru the economic issue is the overmastering thing, and he sees clearly that, as it has grown up, even the Indian National Congress is an expression of the desire of the bourgeoisie to get into their own hands the power now held by the British. He believes in non-violence only as a method right in certain circumstances ; his outlook is in all essentials identical with that of the social revolutionary leaders of other lands, who propose to take every opportunity to secure power that events may offer. There is nothing astonishing in this, and Mr. Nehru's book is so simple and honest that it is impossible not to respect the quality of character there revealed. But we must face the fact that at present many of the keenest and finest spirits are moving toward the social revolution and away from either political co-operation with institutions of British provenance or the mystical ideas of Mr. Gandhi.

Perhaps this is the place to say what has so often been said, that much depends upon the quality of men that Britain can send to India in the different types of service, and upon the disappearance of the still strong

social separateness between Indians and British. I
think that Pandit Nehru is right when he derides the
excessive attention given by certain public men to
the personal element in government—as though Indian history depended upon a gesture here or a conversation there. But it is true, more true than the
pandit will admit, that great harm has been done by
the social exclusiveness of the British. (I was interested to find a new line being taken by Indians about
the question of exclusion from clubs: European society, it is now said, is overrated and the clubs not
worth joining!) The tragedy of it is that there is
nothing rare or difficult about Indo-British friendship; the two peoples seem to have been made for
each other, and no race on earth has a deeper affection to give to those whom it takes to its heart than
has the Indian. Something of that power of affection
to transmute the public scene was manifested at the
time of the death of the late king. When the news
arrived in India shops began to shut immediately, by
the spontaneous action of the people themselves. In
Calcutta, at the time of the memorial services in the
churches, two immense processions moved from the
heart of the Indian city to the *maidan,* or public
park : one of Hindus and one of Moslems. A Hindu
judge of the high court headed one procession, barefoot and clothed in Hindu funeral raiment. He was
joined en route by the Maharaja of Burdwan, also
barefoot. The feeling of personal loss was evident on
all hands, and the different parties seem to have felt
that they were united with one another and with the
British and the government in something that wholly
transcended politics.

One aspect of the political stalemate and disillusionment is the rise of the communal problem. I believe that in the long run the antagonism of the communities—Hindu and Moslem, Sikh and Moslem, Brahman and non-Brahman—will be dissolved by the rise of new groupings based on genuinely political or economic differences ; to some extent already the communal acerbity has disappeared within the nationalist movement. But in the main the Congress is Hindu. The great Moslem territorial magnates are outside it, and since the communal award of the British prime minister in 1931 there has been a party of ardent Hindus whose determination to oppose the award is so great that they have pursued their activities apart from the Congress, which has on the whole honestly tried to look beyond communal allegiance. It is easy to exaggerate the strength of this communal spirit, but there are some facts to be kept in mind. One is the power of religious animosity when two widely different religions, such as Hinduism and Islam, sway a mass of illiterate people among whom there are other lines of cleavage which roughly coincide with the religious. Hindus have a real horror of cow killing, and Moslems a real contempt for idolatry, but the dangers of popular rioting are greater if there is simultaneously present an agrarian issue, with landlords of one faith and tenants of the other, or if, as in the Panjab, a great deal of the land debt is owed by Moslems to Hindus. I think it is fair also to say that when once the fateful decision is made (as, *pace* the Indian National Congress, I believe it has been made) to transfer power by stages to a popularly elected Indian legislature, there is certain to be a long period of maneuvering for power. Some Hindus deeply believe that nothing is really Indian in India but the Hindu tradition and that the other communities are, as it was unwisely put not long ago, " guests." Moslems, in the face of that, do begin to doubt whether their own type of culture will get a fair chance to survive. Hindus, on the other hand, cannot help taking notice of the statements of some Moslem publicists who seem to think or dream only of an all-Moslem empire, in which a part of India would be included.

But there is a certain amount of sheer insincerity about the whole business. The name of religion is invoked to cover purely secular animosities. There was in the Panjab when I was there in the spring a great Sikh-Moslem crux, widely debated everywhere, over certain property at Shahidganj. To judge by their public utterances you would gather that for each community the property under debate was unspeakably sacred, but I was told by two prominent men, one of each party, that the place had at certain times been used as a latrine by each community. They were, in fact, engaging in a trial of strength before the new reforms came in, and religion offered an excellent *casus belli*.

It is this sort of thing that leaves one with the feeling that much of Indian political life is unreal, and that (here I agree with Pandit Jawaharlal Nehru) the real issues in a country so poor, so illiterate and so tightly held by vested interests are social and economic. In certain respects the general economic position of India is good ; her budget is balanced and her trade figures compare favorably with those of most of the world.   But the country people have been through a terrible time in the depression, and the no-rent movement in the United Provinces, while taken up warmly by the Congress, was not primarily political but based upon the tragic condition of things in the rural areas of that great region.   Doctors say that tuberculosis is increasing in India, at a time when in the West we are learning to conquer it ; the reason seems to lie chiefly in malnutrition.   I heard in Bengal of peasants reduced to eating boiled jute fiber.   Rural debt is so great in some provinces that it is difficult to see how it can ever be discharged. Fortunately there is no lack of evidence that the government, headed by the viceroy, whose personal interest in rural questions is widely known, is awake to these issues.   The avoidance of an agrarian revolution in the future depends, I feel, not only upon certain additions being made to the amenity and the efficiency of rural life, but also upon firm dealing with vested interests, some of which are deeply entrenched in Indian society.

There is everywhere a steady increase of concern about rural issues.   The terrible illiteracy (even today not 10 per cent of the population can read and write) is recognized as something that can be and ought to be removed.   If Dr. James Yen could say what he did about China,[2] it is hard to see why anything less should be expected in India.   Here is one of the obvious opportunities for technique to come to the aid of good will.   Much more is known in the world as a whole about the best way to teach reading, both to children and to adults, than was known a

[2] See p. 52.

few years ago, and it can be made available for the masses of Asia. Dr. Laubach [3] has shown in the Philippines what amazing things can be accomplished when a good method is joined to resolution and enthusiasm. Such workers as Dr. and Mrs. Harper at Moga in the Panjab have shown in their own sphere what inroads can be made upon illiteracy when the resources of the modern world are used. Of course, illiteracy is only one of a mass of evils—debt, drink, disease, superstition—under which the village labors, but no real advance among the people is possible unless the burden of illiteracy is lifted.

But I do not think that anyone will deny that the chief factor in the Indian rural situation in recent years has been the rise of a new consciousness among the untouchables, or depressed classes, numbering some fifty or sixty millions. The fundamental thing is that among these poor people themselves, not merely among others who care about them, a new determination has been born. Future historians will, I think, put much of this down to the credit of Mr. Gandhi, and it is indeed ironical that now, when his own labors in their behalf have helped to awaken them, they should be turning against the Hinduism of which he is so ardent and wholehearted a champion.

Mr. Gandhi calls the untouchables *harijans* or " men of God," meaning, I think, that they are specially dear to God. I have no shadow of doubt that in this matter Mr. Gandhi's own deepest convictions and emotions are engaged. For him the evil of untouchability—I have heard him refer to those who are not only " untouchable " and " unapproachable "

[3] See *International Review of Missions*, April, 1936.

but " unseeable "—is no true part of Hinduism ; he would cease to be a Hindu tomorrow if he believed it were, and therefore it is for him a task both of compassion and of religious uprightness and truth to convince caste Hindus that they are wrong in holding to the idea and practice of untouchability, and to claim for the *harijans* the rights of Hindus.   He has also combined his zeal for the use of homespun cloth and the resuscitation of village industries with his concern for the *harijans,* and the Indian Village Industries Association is his instrument for carrying his ideas broadcast through India.   It is, of course, closely linked with Congress, and is for that reason the object of much suspicion on the part of the government.

While it is foolish to decry Mr. Gandhi's efforts in this matter or to fail to recognize his burning sincerity, the results of the campaign have not been very encouraging.   It is true that the untouchables' case has now become a first-rate issue in Indian public life. The method of stimulating social reform by occasional fasts is open to criticism, but it has the advantage, when employed by someone as much beloved by the mass of Indians as Mr. Gandhi, that it arrests universal attention.   Everyone knew that Mr. Gandhi was fasting in protest against the untouchables' being given a separate electorate, as the prime minister's award had decided.   In the stress of public emotion caused by the fast the orthodox Hindu leaders agreed to new arrangements whereby, within the parliamentary seats reserved for Hindus, special provision was made for the election of representatives of the untouchables.   This was the gist of the Poona Pact, the terms of which Dr. Ambedkar, the untouchables' leader, has been so anxious to preserve even if the untouchables should abandon Hinduism. Probably no one else but Mr. Gandhi could have achieved so much in the time, faulty as the pact has since been shown to be. But inquiry in outcaste areas and among those deeply concerned with the issue does not reveal as great an advance as might be expected. There is a certain amount of spectacular inter-dining, new wells have been dug, schools have been opened to untouchables—all very much to the good. What remains doubtful is whether any true and deep change has come about in the Hindu mind.

Dr. Ambedkar, the representative of the depressed classes at the third Round Table Conference, is in no doubt that Hindus cannot and will not substantially change. He accordingly announced, in a speech in October, 1935, at Nasik near Bombay, that he would not die a Hindu, and advised the depressed classes to follow his lead. He, like Mr. Gandhi, is sincerely concerned with the well-being of the depressed classes or " exterior castes." Mr. Gandhi believes that the way lies in purifying Hinduism ; Dr. Ambedkar thinks that Hinduism is by nature incapable of decisive repentance, and that the only thing for the untouchables to do is to leave it.

In a sense, it is now up to the caste Hindus. If Mr. Gandhi is right, and the " exterior castes " deeply desire to remain Hindu, which is their birthright and their historic faith, then the caste Hindus' duty is obvious. Let them abolish untouchability, open the temples and uplift their sunken brethren. If they do not respond, Dr. Ambedkar's case is proved. He for his part seems to be a practical-minded person, not much interested in the theoretical statements of divines about what the religions they expound ideally stand for. He is concerned with the social well-being of his community and attaches great importance to the political gains recently achieved by him on their behalf. The present position appears to be this. Dr. Ambedkar has repeatedly said that while he is determined to leave Hinduism he does not yet know to what spiritual home he would advise his friends to resort. Meetings are being held in different parts of India at which the untouchables are urged to break with Hinduism. At Lucknow in May there was held a " Depressed Classes Conference " at which in addition to their own discussions the delegates listened to speeches by the representatives of several religions. It is more than doubtful whether such meetings are of any value. This one was packed with Moslems who shouted down some of the non-Moslem speakers ; this did the Christian speakers, in particular, no harm in the eyes of the untouchables, and their speeches were dignified and truly religious, but it is an unseemly way in which to approach religious questions.

In August, 1936, a sensation was caused by the publication [4] of correspondence between Dr. Ambedkar and Dr. Moonje, the president of the Hindu Mahasabha, which is the political organization of Hinduism. Dr. Moonje undertook that if Dr. Ambedkar would lead his followers into the Sikh fold

[4] The papers were communicated to the press by Mr. M. C. Rajah, a rival of Dr. Ambedkar for the leadership of the untouchables and a champion of Mr. Gandhi's approach to the question.

the Hindus would accept this, and would press the government to extend the political provisions for the representation of the untouchables (gained in the Poona Pact) to these classes as " Neo-Sikh " ! Dr. Ambedkar's supporting memorandum took the surprising line of argument that while either Islam or Christianity would be better than Sikhism for the outcastes, considered from their point of view, yet the interests of Hinduism and the Hindu culture in India pointed to Sikhism. Islam or Christianity, he felt, would denationalize the untouchables ; for them to become Moslems would mean Moslem domination, to become Christians would strengthen British rule. Sikhism was within the ambit of Hindu culture ; let the Hindus recognize this and make up the financial limitations of the Sikhs whose own help to the untouchables could be but small.

The full meaning of this curious episode is not yet clear, and it is possible that they are right who still claim that Dr. Ambedkar has a fuller appreciation of the meaning of religion than his involuntary revelations would indicate. What *is* of immense significance is the fact that a man in Dr. Moonje's position should be convinced that the untouchables cannot be held within Hinduism except in a vague cultural sense.

Behind these machinations there are afoot movements among the people far deeper and more extensive than any we have known in recent years in India. It is a good many years since Bishop Whitehead of Madras compared the Indian mass movement toward Christianity with the labor movement in England, as an uprising of the underprivileged in the determination to claim the place due to them as human beings. It is an apt comparison, and even more so now that there is something stirring among the out-castes wider even than the mass movement into the church—with which I shall deal a little later.

One proof of the wide extent of this outcaste move-ment and its independence of any one leader such as Dr. Ambedkar is to be found in the phenomenon of the Ezhavas' movement in southwestern India. Here is a community of about a million (estimates vary), not technically untouchable though prevented from entering the temples, possessing in its upper strata a certain number of professional men. This entire community is " on the move." It has differences with the Hindus, partly religious, partly social, partly po-litical ; they are old and deep-seated, and the com-munity has possessed leaders who have gradually developed within it a keener corporate determina-tion than in the groups of untouchables proper in the rest of India. I should greatly doubt whether Dr. Ambedkar's action has had anything at all to do with these Ezhavas' determination to move. This mass feeling, compounded of many grievances, is slow to reach expression-point, but when it has at last done so it will be slow to die away. It is this that makes the increasing tendency of Indian depressed groups to move away from Hinduism so important and im-pressive. It looks as though only a great, immediate and widespread reform within caste Hinduism could change it.

How is it with Indian religion ? Are there signs of that inward renewing in Hinduism and Islam which might enable them to meet the new time of testing ?

The backbone of Hinduism is the village caste life. It has gone on for centuries in the same way ; it is immensely tough, for it is not a doctrinal system nor a code of ethics, but the totality of the varied culture of an ancient people dwelling in half a million villages. The only definition of Hinduism that I have ever heard that seemed to cover the facts was given by a Hindu : " A Hindu is one who, having been born in caste, calls himself a Hindu." But while there is no central dogma and no focal historical fact by his relation to which a man's Hinduism can be tested, there is a whole mass of cults, doctrines and practices which together compose what one might call the Hindu atmosphere. Such are caste, reincarnation and the law of karma (cause and effect inexorable in the moral sphere), respect for Brahmans, worship of some at least of a pantheon of deities, reverence for the cow, and so on. I know of no definite proof that this village Hinduism is changing, but I am certain that it is being subjected, even in the villages, to influences that must change it. The motor bus brings the villager into the country town and the town into the village. The severe economic pressure drives doctors and lawyers more and more into the villages, because they cannot all make a living in the towns. As the pressure on the land increases—and this is one of the major results of the decay of hand industries—more and more people have to go to the mines and the mills to work. They come back different, just as the tribesman goes back from the Rand or the copper mines of Rhodesia to his village a different man. They have been in the wider world, and the religion they know, with its moral sanctions and taboos, be-

longs to the village and the simpler conditions where
caste could be kept and a man knew his gods and
their trees and holy places.

It is in the greater centers that we must look to see
if there be any readjustment of Hinduism to meet
the claims of a new world. Take Benares, the great
city of pilgrims and temples and the holy Mother
Ganges. It is not easy to discern any signs of change
there. Is there in all the world any holy place that
more powerfully appeals to the sense of compassion ?
Who that has seen it can forget the crowded bathing-
ghats, the streams of pilgrims, the multitude of
priests, the pride of the Brahmans, the squalor of the
temples ? There is true religious yearning here, as
the Christian workers who spend their days in continuous talk with the pilgrims can testify, but no essential change in what Hinduism offers. In Benares
there is a university, which among other glories possesses as good scientific laboratories, especially in elec-
trical engineering, as there are in India. There are in
the place devout men, who use to the full such appa-
ratus of religious growth as orthodox Hinduism affords, but the contrast between the modern scientific
teaching and the naïvely orthodox Hinduism of the
pandits is too great for the students, and they turn
from religion with derision. They may still be keenly
communal—though on the whole it is not the young
who fan the fires of communal hatred—but communal loyalty is not religion, as we know well enough
in the West. Yet they will turn out in hundreds to
hear the Christian message preached by such a man
as Dr. Stanley Jones. The only sign of radically new
development within Hinduism that I have heard of

in Benares is the new temple of Mother India—containing simply a marble relief map of India and no other symbol of worship.

The two " acids of modernity " that are eating into orthodox Hinduism are industrialism and education. Each of the great industrial areas is a maelstrom of humanity in which the cults and distinctions that are the essence of day-to-day Hindu living can no longer be maintained. Instead, there comes into the workman's mind, perhaps, some glimmering of new and intoxicating doctrine, of the leveling of distinctions and the abolition of priests and all the paraphernalia of religion that prevent the coming of the people's rule. The industrial regions of India are not large, and although India is one of the eight major industrial countries and has more people employed in industry than the whole population of Spain, numerically these are only a fraction of the masses of the people. But they are an important fraction, for they, just as much as the Western-educated man, have in their own way been drawn into the orbit of Western civilization.

The other disintegrating force is that of education, and it is unnecessary to elaborate here a point which is familiar to all. Macaulay was wrong in thinking that education would by itself destroy idolatry, and he shared to the full in the naïveté of his time, which underestimated the historic strength of the Hindu system and too easily identified Christianity and the Western learning. But he was right in holding that Western education was essentially revolutionary in its relation to Hinduism. The ordinary young educated man in India—and this is becoming more and

more true of young women also—is without religion.
The head of one of the best known student hostels in
India, resorted to by an able type of man, told me
that he did not think that a single one of his students
had any religious sense at all.

In times of great national exaltation, especially in
the common enduring of hardship, such men turn
back to religion. I have suggested that that is happening in China now. But the spirit of disillusionment of which I wrote above does not help in the
growth of religion. Nationalism sometimes has
taken to itself some of the power and emotional
content of religion, and one finds periods when Hinduism is tacitly restated under the influence of nationalist fervor, every good thing from whatever quarter
being dutifully discovered within it. I may be
wrong, but I do not feel that that is happening now
in India very much. The men whom the young educated people follow do not care for religion. Pandit
Jawaharlal Nehru, for all his love and admiration of
Mr. Gandhi, is obviously at a loss to know what he
means by his insistent appeals to religion. On the
other hand, we have such movements as the self-
respect movement in south India which, beginning
as a protest against the privileges of Brahmans, went
on to develop along militantly antireligious lines,
and now aims equally at the spreading of social reform and the abolition of religion.

It is said by Moslem leaders—it was said to me by
some distinguished ones—that this is, if true, at least
much less true of the educated younger Moslems.
They have a more definite dogmatic faith to adhere
to, and there are plenty of "modernist" Islamic

scholars who are offering an Islam attuned to modern needs. But in such a place as Aligarh it would be difficult, if I may judge by what I am told, to find much real Moslem devotion, whatever the loyalty to Islam as a community.

And yet I believe it would be a profound mistake to underestimate the possible recuperative power of the old religions. Hinduism especially has shown again and again in its history how it can rise up in unsuspected power and embrace and absorb the new factor or the threatening obstacle. It can never do that to true Christianity, for reasons that we shall examine later, but it not only can but quite certainly will do just that to any pseudo-Christianity that deserts the foolishness and stumbling block of the cross to commend itself more pleasantly to Hindu minds.

It has been my own conviction, based on such studies as I have been able to make, that Hinduism, because of its failure to treat history seriously or to do justice to personality either in God or in man, must always fail in the long run to provide the moral dynamic that India needs. I must in honesty say that there are two societies, one purely Hindu and the other virtually so, that seem to contradict this theory. One is the Ramakrishna mission, whose labors both in education and in every kind of social reform are well known in India. In times of famine and flood the Ramakrishna people are in the field always among the first, and some of their schools will compare with the best for educational alertness, self-criticism and efficiency. The other society, less well known, is that of the Radhasoamis at Agra, with branches in other parts of the country. I had the privilege of a talk with his holiness, the head of the society, and was, like others who have studied its activities, immensely impressed by the variety and quality of educational and industrial work done. Here are people who are based on what, with certain variations, is Hinduism, though they would admit a member who called himself a Christian if he accepted their fundamental doctrines and placed himself under complete obedience to the head. They accept the machine age, differing vigorously in this from Mr. Gandhi. They are consciously trying to meet the concrete economic needs of India as they see them by developing a form of training calculated to produce the right sort of citizens. All this they do, not with an uneasy parade of a religion of which they are more than half uncertain, but definitely out of a corporate religious consciousness.

While, therefore, I should assert that the old Indian religion has lost its *religious* grip on those classes which are most in touch with the modern world of ideas, and has shown little sign of such radical reforming intelligence as would avail to turn the fortunes of the day, we should be foolish to act on the assumption that the older religious culture no longer matters. The Christian movement is in great need of accurate and scholarly knowledge of what is going on within these religions today.[5]

What of Christianity in India ? The Christian approach to India is along many roads. Matters of Christian missionary policy are discussed later ; my purpose here is simply to refer to the things that most

[5] The Henry Martyn School of Islamic Studies, Lahore, is among other things doing this admirably so far as Indian Islam is concerned.

impressed themselves upon me as I went about India early last year. But it is a never ceasing source of wonder to behold the multitude of modes of service and Christian expression that the resourceful spirit of Christian evangelism has brought into being. The village evangelist, the town pastor, the organizer in his office, the doctor, the nurse, the scientific research worker in the hospital, the village teacher, the matron in the boarding school, the public schoolmaster, the college professor, the agricultural expert, the man who superintends cooperative societies, the worker among the factory hands, the man or woman in the city settlement, the writer, the theological teacher, the expert in pedagogy training village teachers, the " rescue " worker, the Christian *sadhu,* the bishop or chief pastor—what an array it is ! There are Indians and missionaries in all these callings, and more. These number only the special workers set apart for service, but the whole Christian approach to India, as to other lands, includes the men and women in every diversity of " secular " occupation who are trying in their separate spheres to practice a true Christian discipleship.

It has often been said that the only possible policy for Christian education in India, as in other countries where an increasing provision is made by the state and by private enterprise, is that it should aim at quality, and be content with a decreasing share in the total quantity of national education. More and more in India, as the church grows it will be found that the principal object of Christian education is to educate Christians. Yet there will be an opportunity for many years to come for Christian schools and colleges, in their different grades, to do some things so well that they give a lead to the country.

In the education of girls and women the Christian forces still do work of the most outstanding quality. It is no longer the case that it is only or mainly Christian girls who want education, or their parents for them ; all the great communities are changing in this respect, most notably in the Panjab, where there has been a rush to the schools on the part of Hindu, Sikh and Moslem girls.

In methods of village primary education and in training teachers for it the best Christian institutions are the best in the country. The newer methods employed at such places as Moga are not followed widely enough even by Christian schools, but a glance at the visitors' book shows to what an extent this place has become an educational Mecca to which not only Christian and missionary but government and other educators resort for inspiration. I doubt whether there is any department of Christian work in India that can show more both of religious alertness and technical efficiency than the best of the centers of rural teacher training. They are full of hope and suggestion for the future. One of the best instances of this resourcefulness that I have seen was in Bengal, where the students at Chapra preparing to be village teachers decided to try the method in their annual camp—hitherto an evangelistic effort on conventional lines and somewhat fruitless—of teaching crafts to the villagers among whom they went. The result was that normally inaccessible people not only welcomed this unexpected help but insisted on asking why such help was spontaneously rendered. " Who pays you ? Why do you come ? " The students found that their use of the crafts they were themselves learning brought them into intimate touch with the villagers, and gave them an opening that they had never had before to explain what the love of Christ meant to them.[6]

In no aspect of missionary work in India has there been more obvious advance in recent years than on the rural side. The idea of a coherent plan, in which church and school, hospital and credit bank all join with the home in the building of a Christian rural society, has been widely accepted. When it is remembered how vital to India is the conquest of illiteracy, and how necessary it is for the fight against illiteracy to be waged as a part of a wider program of rural " uplift," it is plain that these rural Christian units that have arisen out of the experiments of recent years are going to play a very great part in the future.

Another new development which seems to me to be of far-reaching importance is the closer linking of the Christian colleges with the community, especially the villages. The Lindsay commission on the Christian colleges suggested that what it styled " extension and research " should be an integral part of the life of every college. By this it meant a double process : on the one hand, bringing into the consciousness of the staffs, and through them of the students, the needs of the community, so that by the continuous endeavor to face the questions that arise out of the community life there should be an attack on the examination-fetish and the deadening of spirit that goes with it ; on the other, making available for the community

[6] See article by the Rev. Frank Ryrie in the *International Review of Missions* for July, 1936.

—the village teachers and pastors, for instance—
something of the knowledge that is the possession of
a center of Christian learning.[7]   Put thus, the plan
may sound very abstract.   But if it is considered in
relation to the great movement of the depressed
classes towards the church, of which I shall have more
to say in this chapter, I think it becomes luminously
clear.   If there is going to be an even greater growth
of the village churches in the next five years than any
period in the last century has known, all sorts of questions will have to be faced that will tax to the utmost
the brains and ability of the whole church.   Problems of education, of church development, of the
relation between the functional organization of a
Hindu community, with its caste groupings, and the
Christian society—these and many more will have to
be faced.   The more closely the Christian colleges
can be linked with the church in facing these issues,
the better.   It is not necessary that such liaison work
should have only the Christian community in view,
though it is right that the colleges should use first
the natural links they have with the Indian church.
Christians in the villages are a part of the total social
organism, and it would be alien to the genius of the
Christian religion to seek to promote a Christian communal spirit.   An excellent instance of the touch of
college on community was shown me in the Panjab
by Mr. Heinrich, who is working in a Panjab village
in connection with the Forman Christian College,
Lahore.   Of all the interesting and stimulating things
I learned from him none was more suggestive than

[7] *Report of Commission on Christian Higher Education in India*,
p. 159 ff.

his story of the cup he has persuaded someone to offer for the cleanest village in the district. It was usually won, at first, by the Christian village where Mr. Heinrich works, but there was great joy this year when for the first time a Moslem village got the cup. A rivalry of this sort is the best possible antidote to the communal virus.

I have begun what I have to say of the Christian movement in India with these matters, for although by far the most notable thing in India from the Christian point of view is the turning of whole communities to Christ, it would be wrong to consider that apart from any insight into the most living and developing factors in the Christian church as it now is. Let us now look at the evangelistic opportunity.

Next only to the movement among the depressed classes I should place in significance the marked enhancement of the evangelistic spirit within the Indian church. It is very easy for people in the West who look out upon India or China from a great distance to take an utterly unreal view of the indigenous churches. It is habitually assumed that churches in the " mission field " will manifest continually a level of devotion, sacrificial giving and evangelistic power that is virtually unknown in the Christian West. The Indian Christians, especially the more educated among them, are in touch with the tendencies of thought and life in the modern world. The same things that diminish evangelistic power in Western communions affect them ; they face the same problems, wrestle with the same doubts. They get their problems a little later, and they have on the whole less experienced help in dealing with them—no one who has not been a missionary really knows what understaffing means—but they are in the same world. A good many of the best men I have known in India have faced just the same doubts as the rest of us.   In what does the unique element in the gospel consist ? Is the inspiration of the Scriptures, critically considered, something different from that of the Bhagavad Gita, and if so, wherein exactly lies the difference ? Other questions arise also of a more Indian provenance.   With a largely illiterate church—the percentage of literacy is about 28—is it really good that these masses of outcastes should be brought in ?   Even as things are, the rate of literacy in the church is declining because of them.   Is it fair—this doubt affects especially those of nationalist temper—to Mr. Gandhi and the better Hinduism to take in numbers of depressed class converts when efforts are being made to alter the Hindu attitude ?   Is the church really vital to the gospel, or is it something Western, not necessarily to be taken over into India which has her own adoration of the Christ?   I could say much more of all this, but this may indicate the kind of problems that arise, and, I would add, must inevitably arise if Christians are alive and think.

Having noted these things I can say with all the more force that the leadership in the present evangelistic movement is emphatically Indian.   The National Christian Council, representing virtually all the missions and churches in India except those of Rome, has launched a five years' movement of evangelism, and it is most impressive to see how earnestly it is being taken up by pastors and clergy and lay leaders everywhere. I obtained ample proof of this as I went about. There is an atmosphere of conviction and of being possessed by a message. I felt it most when at Nagpur I met with a group of Indian clergy and ministers who had come together to talk over the interests of their work. They were not, with one or two exceptions, outstanding men, but all were responsible leaders such as represent the life of the church better than those of quite unusual gifts. I think that anyone who could have listened to those conversations would have felt extraordinarily encouraged about the future of the church in India. I have just been looking through my notes of what they said. They were in every case conscious that there lay before them an opportunity greater than they had ever known. This consciousness was expressed quite as strongly by men who came from such centers as Benares where difficulties are almost overwhelming as by those who were already grappling with the mass movement of the untouchables. A city pastor from the north gave an account of how the members of his church had carried out the week of witness, which in all parts of India has been a constituent part of the new evangelistic forward movement. A man from the central provinces was on fire with what he and others had found in the endeavor to apply the principles of Dr. Pickett's mass movement study to that area : whole communities were found ready and anxious to be taught and received. Another told how the Madras churches had raised from their own resources money to send him as a missioner into the congregations of the farther south. Another told us how he had been in friendly touch with the Arya

Samajists—probably the most definitely and militantly anti-Christian group in the whole of Hindu society—and had actually been invited to address a meeting of ten thousand of their members. One got the impression of men who were not trying to heighten effects by exaggeration, or were blind to the immense difficulties by which they were faced, but who were sure of their message and felt themselves to be in the service of a triumphant Lord.

My own impressions, for what they are worth, coincide entirely with what these men had to tell. I noticed that in some of the most difficult areas of north India, where the church has always been very small relative to the great populations, there were indications of a movement. The kind of man who has always been willing to discuss and inquire was now facing decision, and often making it.

This is the true setting in which to see the turning of the depressed classes. This, again, is not a new thing. At least 80 per cent of the Christians in India of the non-Roman communions (it is possible that the same is true of the Roman Church) have come directly or at one or two removes from the untouchables or depressed classes. In the Panjab the Christian population has increased tenfold in thirty years. In the Dornakal diocese in the Telugu country, when Bishop Azariah first went there in 1919, there were 86,000 Christians ; at the end of 1935 there were over 200,000, of whom 11,000 had been baptized during the year. It is estimated that in the last two years over 112,000 persons have been baptized through the labors of the seven principal missions in the Telugu country. Bishop Azariah has 40,000 people who are

ready and willing to be taught, but he cannot supply
teachers.

Most significant of all, the community movement
has now become in the Telugu country not only a
movement of untouchables—Malas and Madigas,
themselves deeply divided by communal feeling—
but a movement among the caste people. It is estimated that about 60,000 people of the Sudra castes
(below the Brahmans and above the untouchables—
the middle castes of rural Hinduism) have become
Christians in that region. I asked a group of Indian
clergy, rural deans in the diocese of Dornakal, what
in their experience it was that brought the Sudras to
Christ. They all answered in the same language as
others had used : "They have seen the change in
the depressed class Christians." Nowhere can one
better see the church alive and witnessing, itself by
its life carrying the evangel.

Into this India and this kind of Christian preparation come now the restless millions of untouchables.
I have already said that the motives with which they
look away from Hinduism to other faiths are mixed,
and it is inevitable in the nature of the case that they
should be mixed. Can anyone conceive a great
movement making itself felt among millions of back-
ward illiterate folk, who have seen a glimpse of freedom and a better human standing in the world,
without embracing a mixture of motives ? Let it be
fully recognized that we have not before us a religious movement of spiritual awakening and longing
for Christ, so much as a deep restlessness and a determination to find the way to freedom. But the leaders
of the untouchables are well aware that without the

strength of religion the goals they desire must forever be unattainable by their people. What folly to talk of detaching the untouchables from Hinduism, if that were to be all!

I suppose that the turning, not only away from Hinduism, but toward Christianity, has gone furthest with the Ezhavas in Travancore and the Malayalam-speaking region. At a little conference of leaders of four churches with whom I met at Alwaye, one Indian clergyman told of a meeting between some Ezhava leaders and some Christians, at which the Ezhavas put forward four points as matters on which they were convinced: " We are disgusted with Hinduism. We admire what we know of the teaching and character of Jesus Christ. We admire the lives of the missionaries we have met. We admire the philanthropic work, such as schools and hospitals, carried on by the missions and we think that all these things are good for our people."

The latest news that I have seen from Travancore suggests that the Ezhavas are not going the length immediately of offering en masse to become Christian—of which there was some fear after their votes in community meetings. They are determined to leave Hinduism ; the next steps they leave to be settled later. The same thing was true in the conference of untouchables held in May at Lucknow. It is infinitely better that it should be so, for there is then a spirit of inquiry and expectancy aroused and it is possible for the ordinary activities of the Christian church, reinforced, let us hope, and made fully coherent and united, to be brought to bear all over India on this moving and seeking people.[8]

[8] On all this see *The Untouchables' Quest*, by G. E. Phillips.

When in a later chapter we come to discuss some of the problems of upbuilding the church throughout the world we shall return to the needs that this great movement lays upon us all. I want to end this account of things seen in India—an account full of contradictions—by recording my own deep sense of the relentless opposition which will be offered by Hinduism to the great Christian ingathering which may be upon us. Let no one imagine that the tolerance of Hinduism, its amorphous character theologically considered, its ability to admire all religious types and to include them if they will, spells a tolerance of evangelism which has as its end baptism and the integrated life of the Christian church. Of this Mr. Gandhi is himself the best possible example, for he has drunk deeply of Christian inspiration while remaining intensely Hindu. Mr. Gandhi is always polite, but he can hardly speak with kindness of the Christian work for the outcastes in medical and educational succor and social betterment, because the Christians persist in offering also the Christian religion. For him it means using a bait to proselytize ; for us it is the sheer duty to give not only learning and health and solvency—good things but none of them absolutes—but the knowledge of God's love in Christ.

In this Mr. Gandhi will prove typical of Hinduism, and it is well that we should recognize it. A significant incident occurred lately in the United Provinces' legislative council. In conference with the Indian Christian leaders the minister of education had admitted that it was reasonable that special educational grants made to the depressed classes should not be withheld from Christians of those groups whose economic condition still united them with those from whom they had come. The grants were based on economic condition, not on community, so that this view was obviously just. In the council, however, a storm arose, and the minister was compelled to accept a motion removing the grant, on the ground that it was a subsidy to proselytism.

There is a jealous conscience among Indian Christian leaders on this matter of proselytism, and missionaries need no urging to abstain from the appearance of unworthy solicitation and use of material gain as a stimulant. No one who really knows anything at first hand ever repeats these stories ; if there were nothing else to say, at least it is plain that the missions are too badly hit financially to be able to bribe the population of India ! But my point is this, that *even if every unfair method is avoided,* there is no acceptance by Hinduism of the fundamental right of conversion. The same tolerance that leads the inquirer to admire easily and to say meditatively, " Yes, all religions teach the same," comes round full circle with a great hatred of that religion which in the name of its Lord and Master *must* be exclusive and *must* demand total surrender, and cannot claim less for him than that he is Lord of all and that in him are all things fulfilled. Here, in this assertion of the unshared lordship of the Lord, is the *skandalon,* the stumbling block in India. If we did not experience that opposition, we ought indeed to fear.

I V

THE NEAR EAST

TO PASS directly from the crowded Indian scene
with its immense hopes and problems to the totally different countries of the Near East is to pass
from one world to another. My boat took me from
Bombay to Suez; it was full of India, and my mind
was full of India too. From Suez to Cairo by train,
and then a world utterly different from that which I
had left—no mass movements, no Hinduism, the all-
pervading fact of Islam, but nationalism still, and the
rationalist skeptical tone of modern civilization.

My stay in Egypt and Palestine was entirely taken
up with two meetings which, very fortunately, enabled me to make contact with a considerable number of people from different parts of the Near East—
Egypt, Turkey, Iran (formerly but now no more
called Persia), Iraq, Syria and Palestine. One was
the annual meeting of the Egypt Inter-Mission Council; the other that of the executive committee of the
Near East Christian Council, a body that unites in
voluntary cooperation many of the Christian organizations at work in the great area between Iran and
Morocco, Rumania and the southern Sudan. This
region of the earth has never been united as a whole
since the Roman Empire, which comprised it all except the far-distant Parthia; it is divided today
among an extraordinary variety of governments—

national sovereignties, mandates, protectorates and the conditioned independence of Egypt. But it has in common the great fact of Islam, and also, though less evidently, the memory of ancient conflicts in the days when Christendom and Islam represented rival civilizations that waged a secular warfare. Of those older days the ancient Christian churches are a reminder in almost all of these lands—Egypt, Palestine, Syria, Turkey, Iraq and Iran ; but not in northern Africa, from which the church of Augustine and Tertullian has disappeared as completely as Carthage.

I think that the cause of Christian evangelization is confronted with greater obstacles in this area than in any other in the world—I do not, of course, include in this statement " closed " lands such as Tibet proper and Afghanistan, but the countries in which, as in much of the Near East, organized missionary activity has been carried on for two or three generations. These difficulties are all attributable to two causes—the existence of the conception of the Moslem church-state, with the conception of personal law that flows from it, and the strength of nationalism. But these two causes are opposed to one another in principle, and it is the war between them that makes the Near East so fascinating a subject of study. It is possible to discern in the events of common life and political development a continuous struggle between two conceptions of human society that have totally different origins and are in essence completely opposed.

To understand the Moslem church-state we have to go rather further back than most of the argument of this book has taken us.[1] The state which the prophet Mohammed had in mind and which did actually exist under his immediate successors can be justly termed a " church-state." It consisted of church members and those only, and they viewed the existence and activities of their state theologically. It embraced those Arabs who had accepted Islam and had thus separated themselves into a community apart from other Arabs and from the rest of the world. All previous family ties, enmities, feuds, confederations were blotted out ; the new Moslem must accept as a brother in the faith all other Moslems ; the multitudinous feuds of the Arab tribes were now merged in one great feud of the Moslem Arabs against the non-Moslem Arabs, the *Jihad*. This holy war, or better holy feud, springs directly from the old Arab relationship of tribal feud and is the permanent relationship between the Moslem community and all communities that have not accepted Islam. This relationship was transferred from Arabia to the wider world. Arabia had become one and Moslem, and had then poured out into that wider world in the great Arab conquests. Even after the rush of that onset had been stayed it was still recognized as the duty of the caliph of the time (the word caliph means " successor," i.e., the successor of the prophet) to lead an expedition at least once a year against the surrounding non-Moslem states. Later on, when Byzantium held out, and the Pyrenees in the west defined the bounds beyond which in Europe Islam

[1] In the succeeding pages I have relied mainly upon an unpublished paper of the great Christian authority in Islamic studies, D. B. Macdonald.

should not pass, the relations of Christendom and Islam became more settled ; but the obligation of the permanent situation was always recognized.

The difference between Moslem and non-Moslem was, therefore, the basis of constitutional government. To a Moslem professor of canon law the distinction between state and church would be meaningless. The Moslem state originated in prophetic theocracy—that is to say, it was founded by someone who believed himself to be laying down the foundations of the state under the immediate direction of God. The administration of the state is in theory democratic, but this means only that the Moslem people administers a divine system. The constitution and the laws are of divine origin, and in the strict sense there can never be for Moslems any human legislation. The Moslem people determines by its agreement what the divinely given constitution and laws are, and it applies them by its right of administration. Thus the people must, by the very nature of the case, be all Moslems. There is, strictly speaking, no clergy in Islam, so that one line of development into a distinction between church and state is barred. Some Moslems are better educated than others and therefore have a better right to judge, determine and interpret what the divine law and usage are, but there is no further distinction.

The participation of non-Moslems as full citizens in the administration of the state and any new legislation are therefore equally impossible. This has been always the orthodox theory, and the accommodations of this theory to the practical necessities in which Moslem governments found themselves situ-

ated have never ranked as anything more than regrettable concessions to necessity in a world not yet
Moslem. As soon as Islam spread beyond Arabia the
Moslem governments were faced by immovable facts.
Great masses of population were absorbed, non-
Moslem in ideas and usages ; the relative unity of the
Arabian peninsula was left behind for a medley of
civilizations, some highly developed. The populations of the different countries over which Moslem
governments ruled either were Moslem or they were
not ; if they were not, they were either native to the
newly Moslemized territory or they were foreign
colonies settled in these lands for the purpose of
trade. These last the Moslems inherited from the
Byzantine government and treated in just the same
way as the Byzantines had done. The system was
that which, when developed later, came to be known
as the capitulations ; it meant a waiving of sovereignty for the purpose of convenience and to avoid
the trouble of administering alien populations. The
Byzantines also showed the way to deal with the native populations which did not become Moslem.
They had allowed to them large powers of autonomy.
This admirably suited the Moslems, who did not desire the trouble of administering great numbers of
non-Moslems, and must in deference to their own
principles leave them outside the ring-fence of Islam.
As they were not Moslems they could not be citizens,
but were only wards of the Moslem state, with certain
fixed duties toward it in return for a certain protection from it. Their own domestic affairs they could
manage according to their own codes, and the head of
each community—rabbi, patriarch or chief bishop—

was their only link with the Moslem state. The system was never more than a practical accommodation to necessity ; it had no theoretical basis and was alien to Moslem fundamental ideas, but it worked fairly well. In practice it resulted in a series of little states within the state, none with the rights of the Moslem but tolerated and protected and with a definite status. In recent times the capitulations have had a certain influence on the status of these communities and have brought them under a sort of treaty protection.

The part of these alien populations that did embrace Islam had a much deeper effect upon the Moslem state. They formed the bulk of the Moslem populations, and they had their own social usages and ideas. These came to play an ever greater part in the life of the state. Two codes of law gradually appeared : one, the divine code of the theologians and canonists, the revelation of Allah through the Koran and the traditions, developed and codified by human reason and assured by the agreement of the Moslem people ; the other, an admittedly human code based on local customs and necessity, not in Arab lands (of whose customs the first code was a mirror) , but in other countries, and backed by the will of rulers and governments. Between these two codes or provinces of law the boundary is always the same. The canon law rules the personal religious life and duties of the individual and his family life—marriage, divorce, the custody of children, inheritance ; the local codes rule everything else—civil, criminal and commercial law.

It has been a practical division, but it has never been accepted by the theologians, and they have had the support of masses of believing Moslems. It has been a queer but important alliance between the masses and the theologians against the practical administrators and, in these days, the educated classes. Hence the intermittent risings and insurrections; hence the unwillingness of Moslem administrators to take action which may perfectly commend itself to their rational judgment but which they know may rouse the masses against them. Hence, too, the fact that while the Moslem governments used, and were compelled to use, the services of Christian and other non-Moslem officers in the highest posts of their administrations, they dared not ignore the mob, and the Christian official would be foolish if he or his people presumed upon the favor shown them.

There were, then, these three elements always present: the position of the canonists, impregnably entrenched in the divine revelation; the practical administrative situations which governing Moslems had to face; and the masses of the people with their own ideas. Points of friction easily arose when three such elements were present. "Islam in danger" is always a ready cry, and Islam combines two great human interests, patriotism and religion, making them one.

It is not difficult to see why in every country in which Moslem canon law is still the law of personal status Christian missions have been faced by the greatest possible difficulties. Conversion was apostasy, and that was punished by death in the case of men; in the case of women a virtually compulsory marriage was arranged, and it was laid down that in answer to the proposal made, either laughter or tears or silence

was to be taken as consent. (Needless to say, the conversion or apostasy of married women was not even
conceived.) These provisions were of course abro-
gated, at least so far as the death penalty went, in
countries such as Egypt in which an overriding non-
Moslem influence existed in government. In the
same way thieves had not their hands cut off, nor
were adulterers stoned. But whereas provision was
always made, and naturally so, for the registration
and due recognition of converts *to* Islam, none was
made or could be made for conversion *from* Islam.
Moreover, the canon law laid down that a Moslem
cannot inherit from a non-Moslem or vice versa ; a
convert from Islam is *de facto* divorced from his Moslem wife and cannot make a legal will. These conditions mean two things : first, that the work of
evangelism is attended by the most crushing difficulties and that conversion is not merely very unpopular
but outside the legal framework of the life of the
people ; second, that the Christian minority, whether
of converts or of an ancient church, is at a legal dis-
advantage.

I have thought it worth while to set down at length
this Islamic background of principle, for, as we shall
see, it is no mere matter of archeological research but
the statement of doctrines and influences which are
very powerful in Moslem states today. We turn now
to look at the other great influence which is at war
with this idea of the church-state. We are prepared
for it by what has been said of the accommodation of
strict principle to the actual situations in the different
Moslem countries. This is the principle or spirit of
nationalism.

We will begin with Turkey. Here is the champion of the nationalist idea among all the Moslem countries. It is ironical for one who lived in India during the height of the caliphate controversy to reflect how we were told then that it was a religious necessity of Islam that temporal and spiritual power should be united; that Islam knew nothing of the devitalizing distinction between church and state; and that the integrity of the whole of Turkey's possessions, as the home of Islam, was a religious obligation. The Turks, led by Kemal, have driven out the caliph and there is now no commander of the faithful. But they have gone far beyond that. It is hardly too much to say that today Turkey is not a Moslem state in any official sense. She is a secular state in which the bulk of the inhabitants are still in some sense Moslems. The sacred law (Sharia) was abolished, and in its place the Swiss civil code set up. The fez was abolished, though its lack of brim was necessary if good Moslems were to wear their hats at prayer and cause their foreheads to touch the ground. The veil was abolished. The Arabic script vanished and the new Turkish-Roman took its place. Persian and Arabic Scriptures disappeared from the schools; modern European languages were cultivated. The clause which laid it down that " Islam is the religion of the Turkish state " was taken out of the constitution.

Most of this took place fairly soon after the revolution in which the victorious Kemal, fresh from driving the Greeks into the sea, showed himself truly the expression of the mind of his Turkish folk. More recent events include the turning of Santa Sophia into a museum, and the prohibition of clerical dress to all except the actual head of each religious community. This hits the *moulvis* hard, but it also hits hard every other kind of clergyman. Women are now enfranchised, and last year seventeen women were elected to the Grand National Assembly.

Modern Turkey is organized round the idea of race, and of nationality based upon race. It is most significant in this connection to observe that every attempt is being made, especially through the schools, to popularize the idea that the Islamic period of Turkish history is only an episode in the history of the people, and that much importance therefore belongs to the pre-Islamic period of the people's life. I do not know how much significance is to be attributed to the white wolf on the paper money in Turkey —no more, perhaps, than to Britannia and her trident with us in Britain—but I remember seeing in some journal the statement that during the World War Enver Pasha circulated to the troops a prayer to the white wolf, who was a tutelary deity of the Turks on the plains of central Asia. At least the creature suggests an emphasis on the racial history of Turkey to the exclusion of the religious.

The attitude of this reborn Turkish nation—and we must remember the tremendous debt under which Kemal Ataturk has laid his people in rescuing them from the mire of defeat and raising them again to power and unity—toward foreign nations is full of interest. They are to be studied and, where desirable, imitated, but the slightest suspicion of foreign propaganda or attempted domination is the sign for immediate repression. In education there is no doubt whatever that Turkey has set her face toward the West, and that she is determined to be finished with the old predominantly religious Arab-Persian culture. Today it is France and, even more than France, Germany, Britain and America that afford the models in education. I was told some years ago of children's copybooks in which the legends appear for copperplate transcription, " A Turk uses a fork," " A Turk does not eat with his fingers "—very clear suggestion of a desire to turn the current of popular manners toward the West rather than the East. But along with this spirit went a resolute determination to banish the slightest trace of foreign authority. The move to Angora, with the abandonment of Constantinople (Istanbul) as the capital—though there never was a city so obviously destined to be a great capital as Constantinople—was dictated by the resolve to have no more of that overweening foreign diplomacy of which the great city was the symbol. Angora, correspondingly, was the symbol of the free Turkish life of the Anatolian uplands. Again, the ruler would somehow manage without foreign loans, for loans would mean a measure of foreign control ; with enormous difficulty he achieved it, and the production of coal in Turkey (to take only one instance of economic development) reached approximately two million tons in 1935.

How does this secularized nationalist Turkey look upon Christian missions ? Here again the answer depends on factors that are now in the past. Christianity to the Turks has meant, in the main, Armenian and Greek. I have already described the system of " states within the state " by which the sultan's government managed the alien groups. This alone suggested that religion and race-nationality go together, and the whole life of the Near East confirmed the idea. Added to this is the fact that the Turkish government had always regarded the Christian minorities not merely as the object of solicitude by foreign Christian powers but as the spearheads of possible intrigue by those powers.

So much for reaction from the past. But the positive racialism of the present is inevitably, though not perhaps directly, hostile to Christianity. Here we come once more to the totalitarian state and the group of ideas associated with it. It is, I think, clear that Turkey is not interested in Islamic orthodoxy. The sacred Moslem law has gone, and legal ideas of freedom are now taken from the Swiss code and no longer from seventh century Arabia. That ought to mean that there is perfect freedom for conversion. In theory there is, and it is said that instances have been found of individuals or small groups confessing Christ and being defended in their right to do so, against popular local resentment, by official action. But in the main the official desire to banish every kind of foreign propaganda, coupled with the keen determination to instill into the popular mind, and especially into the young, a racial-national gospel, presses very hard upon Christian work. It must be frankly faced that Christianity is at a low ebb in Turkey. It is doubted whether there have ever been so few Christians there for eighteen centuries. The exchange of populations with the Greeks left only a few Greek and Armenian Christians in Istanbul and virtually none in Anatolia ; conversion, as we have

seen, though legally possible is so difficult and unpopular as to be nearly impossible.

Non-Christian pupils may not attend Christian
worship or teaching in Christian schools, even if they
desire to do so. Even the most indirect kind of influence is frowned upon, and the foreign schools are
attacked in the press as centers of foreign culture, denationalizing in their influence. Recently a new
property tax has been imposed upon schools which
were formerly exempt ; it is possible that the tax may
be retroactive, an event which would crush
the foreign schools completely. Publishing is also
suspect : a Turkish translation of Fosdick's *The
Manhood of the Master* was recently confiscated.

The restrictions on " propaganda " are not specifically anti-Christian ; they apply equally to Moslem
propaganda, like the restrictions on clerical dress
and headgear. What matters in the modern Turkey
is Turkishness, the Turkish spirit, belief in the
Turkish destiny. If Islam breathes of the old anti-
scientific priest-ridden world, Christianity savors of
the imperialism of the Western powers. Neither is
adequately Turkish.

In this situation of extreme difficulty the Christian
missions can do little but wait and pray. It is plain
that institutional work will be virtually forbidden to
them. They recognize that they have to convince the
Turks that they have nothing but good will toward
them, and that whether or not it was true in the past,
as the Turks think, that Christianity was tied up
with anti-Turkishness, it is not so now. Some leading Turks have begun to realize this. I was told some

time ago by a friend in Turkey that an official had said to him, " We do not mind your being Protestants so long as you are not Christians " ! [2]   There are groups of young men even in Angora who claim Jesus Christ as their master.   Stories are told of remarkable private gatherings in which Christian discipleship is the inspiring note, but they are not being brought together, and there is a certain fear of resorting to missionaries.   It may be that if such Christians as remain in Turkey can show the needed depth and reality in Christian life, there may yet be an awakening of personal religion and a turning to Christ among Turks.   But the days are dark, and we cannot forget that a militant race-conscious nationalism is no better matrix for Christian love than the Koranic orthodoxy of the old days.

Now let us turn to Iran.   This country has tended in recent years to follow some distance after Turkey but in the same direction.   Here, as in Turkey, the tide of nationalism runs strongly.   Here also is the desire to have done with all that belongs to the picturesque and feeble past, the time when the Westerner looked on the Easterner as a funny person in a picture book.   The hat is changed—hats are an infallible guide to national politics in the Near East— and in place of the old *pahlevi* cap has come the European hat.   The new clothing confers equality on

[2] I ought, perhaps, to explain this remark.   " Christian " meant Greek or Armenian, or French Catholic.   The " Protestants " were Americans, and not regarded in the same light as the emissaries of other nations with different secular relations with Turkey.   But I do not wish to be unfair to the Orthodox and Catholics and have no doubt that the disability of being linked with secular diplomacy is equally obvious and regrettable to them.

all—Iranians, Parsees, Jews, Armenians—; there is no stigma suggested by what a man wears. The unveiling of women has been carried out to completion with relentless severity. The orders came first to girls in government elementary schools, and to their teachers. Then came women inspectors, then girls in private schools. The queen and her daughters drove unveiled through the streets in European dress. Great pressure was brought to bear upon the wives of officials. It was threatened that private schools would be closed unless all the girls unveiled. Veiled women were forbidden to appear in the streets or the cafés, shopkeepers were forbidden to serve them, and finally, the police were empowered to remove the veil from women found veiled in public. These methods are worth noting as indicative of the spirit that informs a determined nationalism which knows what it wants to achieve. It is thought that the total effect may be good, inasmuch as polygamy, already attacked by "advanced" Iranians, is sure to suffer under the new unveiled regime, but there is much sympathy with the older women. Child marriage is already illegal, and the minimum age for a girl to marry is sixteen.

Economic changes have been great. Railways will unite Teheran with the Caspian sea and the Persian (must one say Iranian ?) gulf. Nearly thirteen thousand miles of motor roads have been completed. Iran, like Iraq, has done well in financial negotiation with the West and came off successfully in a legal contest with the Anglo-Iranian Oil Company. There are sugar factories, spinning mills, cement works, fruit-canning industries, woolen mills and leather factories.   Probably at least a thousand Iranian students are studying abroad.

There is a growing spirit of criticism of the older Islamic ways of thought and life.   As in Turkey, much emphasis is placed on the pre-Islamic history of Iran, and the name of the present dynasty (Pahlavi or Parthian) is an index of what is going on.   Archeological research is now having a new effect in creating a fresh interest in the reality of the past.   The critical study of the Koran and the Traditions has begun.   The old Moslem law (Sharia) has been almost set aside, though not formally so as in Turkey. Cases are now determined in the courts according to new codes based on acts of parliament and on direct legislation, without regard to the traditions that have come from the prophet or the imams.   (Iran has always been a Shiah country accepting the imams and not the caliphate.)

The income from religious endowments is being employed by the government for purposes of public welfare.   Numerous theological schools were formerly subsidized by these endowments, but these have now been reduced in number and so changed in character that the students, in addition to accepting a fresh curriculum including studies in science and history, must wear ordinary clothes and submit to gymnastic drill like students in other schools. " An act of parliament was cited in a recent book under the heading : ' Putting out of business uneducated and corrupt theological students who were sycophants and rascals.' " [3]   A sarcastic reflection on

[3] See article " Intellectual Awakening in Modern Iran," by Dr. D. M. Donaldson in the *International Review of Missions*, April, 1936, from which I have drawn in this account of changes in Iran.

the uselessness of the old type of learning and attitude to life is given in an article in a daily paper : " Whenever civilization, inventions and discoveries are discussed, we are sure to hear that God has given this world to the foreigners and the other world to us. . . . We have so many superstitious ideas that we can't move. No matter what happens to us we say ' God is great.' So we sit and hope that one day nature will have pity on us. Other people look on the world from a different angle. They work hard, learn science, and without regarding the angels or devils they do things and make themselves comfortable. We are lost. They have both worlds while we have neither."

In this new Iran the Christian church finds great difficulties set in its way by the keenness of the national spirit, but it is full of courage and hope, for it is convinced that the new spirit of the people enables them to look more fairly than in the past on the Christian teaching. It is in Iran, alone in the Near East, that a church has been built, albeit small, composed mainly of converts from Islam. (There is nowhere in the Near East anything parallel to the situation in east Java where there is a church of thirty thousand people, all of whom have come out of Islam.) There are many public confessions of faith, and it is believed that there is a widespread desire below the surface for Christian confession. The characteristics of the new Moslem converts to the Christian faith are joy and gladness and the desire to tell their friends what has been done for them.

The choice for many of the keenest spirits seems to lie between the abandonment of all religion and the acceptance of Christianity. It seems to have been possible in Iran, more than in certain other Near East countries, to overcome the suspicion that Christianity is necessarily antinational, and there is no doubt of the truly Iranian feeling of the Christians, who believe themselves to be truly Iranian and truly Christian, even though they may have Moslem names. There is therefore much hope among the Christians in Iran.

But this is only one side. There has been continual persecution of missionary schools, sometimes apparently only in the fulfillment of state laws that were aimed at foreign influence especially from Russia, sometimes, it would appear, when an Islamic orthodox influence got into control in official quarters. Missions in Iran live dangerously, with great hope and joy and also with the recognition that a keenly nationalist government, incalculable as all such governments are, might turn them out of Iran tomorrow. But there is a church to continue the work.

From Turkey and Iran, in which the nationalist spirit has on the whole conquered the religiously orthodox, we turn to Egypt, where the situation is very different. Nationalism is a great force in Egypt, but it has run along Islamic channels and there is little antireligious nationalism. The iconoclasm of Turkey has been to Egypt not a beacon to follow but a red light of danger to avoid. She believes that while through all the Moslem centuries Cairo and the Azhar university made Egypt the center of the world of Islam, now more than ever, when Turkey has turned to secularism, must Egypt stand for the Moslem culture. Egypt is in fact torn between two ideals : to be the torchbearer of Islam, and to be in the eyes of Europe a good European. Her political development has been under the influence of Britain, and the denouement now reached in the signing of the Anglo-Egyptian treaty means the establishment of responsible parliamentary government. This is to be done in a country where the Sharia still reigns in the sphere of personal law. The constitution of Egypt states that " Islam is the religion of Egypt," and this has definitely been interpreted to mean that other religious groups must behave as guests and not regard themselves as having the same rights as Moslems.

The problem of the right of conversion has been a grave issue in Egypt for years past. There have been test cases, taken to the courts, which have shown conclusively that whatever modification may be granted privately in individual cases, it is not possible for an unmarried Moslem girl to become a Christian in the sense of securing any legal recognition for the change. The case does not come to the Sharia court as one of conversion, but as a case for the custody of a child, and the result is always the same—the girl is handed over to Moslem guardianship.

The constitution of Egypt, granted in 1922, stated that " liberty of conscience is absolute." We encounter here the fundamental difference that marks off the orthodox Islamic view from that of the Western mind. To any ordinary Western man it would seem axiomatic that " absolute liberty of conscience " included the liberty to change your religion if your conscience led you that way. But to the Moslem it is not so. It means that there is liberty for the Coptic Christian to continue a Copt, for the Armenian to continue an Armenian, for the Jew to continue a Jew. Meanwhile there is provision made by law for the registration of converts from Christianity to Islam, and the pressure of society and of legal advantage is such that the rate of secession to Islam among the Copts, which five years ago was about four hundred a year, is now, I was told, fifteen hundred and likely to rise higher.[4]

It is not, therefore, a matter for surprise that the minorities look to the future with some trepidation. In recent years the Copts have on the whole sided with the Egyptian nationalist movement, and the Wafd party, which has an overwhelming popular hold, numbered several Copts among its leaders. To what extent this arose from a genuine national feeling and to what extent it was due to fear lest an attitude of aloofness might be more dangerous in the long run, it is hard to say. Probably both motives have been present. But the last two years have seen a number of somewhat gross instances of members of the minority communities suffering in the competition for government appointments and in other ways at the hands of the Moslem majority, and there is now much anxiety. But it is a right as well as an inevitable policy that has led to the signing of the treaty, and there is ground for hope that the settling of the long-standing issue between Britain and Egypt may release the constructive energies of the country

---

[4] It is germane to mention here that the number of Englishwomen who have married Egyptian Moslems and become Moslems, mainly under the pressure of legal disability, is increasing.

in such a way as to still the voice of communal
animosity.

But the church-state mentality is still there.   It is
shown not only in the conversion problem but in the
sphere of education.   In the public elementary
schools Moslem teaching was made compulsory and
it was only with much difficulty that the Copts could
secure permission to give Christian teaching to their
children.   Even when this permission had been
granted, it was still only permission to teach in buildings outside the school—though there might be none
available—and the social pressure on the Coptic
parents to send their children to the koranic teaching is very great.   It is pointed out, for instance,
that the lessons are invaluable for the learning of
good Arabic.

While thus hostile to Christian teaching and evangelism, the bulk of Moslem public opinion is pre-
posterously sensitive on the subject of Islam.   The
American University of Cairo, whose standing with
the public has always been very high, is from time to
time assailed because of the existence in its library
of books " defaming Islam," which turn out to be
books of unquestioned and objective scholarship.
The antimissionary press campaign of 1933 was characterized by an amazing depth of credulity in the
things that were said about the methods of missionaries.   One of the commonest charges was the
employment of hypnotism !   But it has always to be
remembered that behind all Egyptian parties lies the
Moslem mob, and no party can afford to have it said
that it is remiss in defending the rights of Islam ; the
safest thing in times of political excitement is to err

in the direction of partisan enthusiasm, and to attack the " evangelists " can never be amiss.

It is, therefore, on all grounds highly to be desired that in the negotiations which attend the entry of Egypt to the League of Nations some such guarantees be given in regard to religious freedom and the treatment of minorities as were given by Iraq at the termination of the mandate.

The orthodoxy of the Azhar, however, is not the whole of Egyptian Islam. There has been for years a struggle within that institution between those who desired to modernize the curriculum and those who stood fast in the old ways. In 1935 the reforming Sheikh el Maraghi was once more installed as rector, and the Council of Ministers has now approved a new set of regulations whereby the modern scientific spirit is to be introduced into all Islamic studies, courses in the comparative study of religion are to be offered, and the knowledge of a foreign language made compulsory. These with certain other reforms mark a complete victory for the " forward " party. Another sign of the times is the decision to have an authorized translation of the Koran made into the English language ; not a literal translation but one designed to convey the real meaning of the book. This proposal was violently attacked as well as defended in the Arabic press.

Egypt, moreover, is being drawn more and more into the world economic order. The great extension of cotton growing has on the whole been socially advantageous to the people, for it has given employment throughout the year and thereby diminished crime. But the keeping of virtually the whole country under water by perennial irrigation, through works stretching from Khartoum to the sea, has tended to spread debilitating disease. As the wealth of the country grows—and cotton has greatly increased it—there are better police protection in the villages, better canals, roads and communications. This has led to a decrease in fanaticism. European dress is being adopted by educated people, especially in the larger towns, as well as by laborers who are in close touch with European technique, as in mechanical occupations. One consequence of this change has been the growth of a tendency to look down upon the sheikhs (religious teachers) as belonging to a lower social class than the effendi (educated man) and this has led to public protests from sheikhs who are obliged to wear robes in their ceremonial and educational duties. Egyptians themselves say that very few educated men pray or fast or indeed think sympathetically at all of religion. But this does not in any way minimize their loyalty to Islam as a community.

Palestine is an example of a totally different form of government from any we have yet described. It is under mandate, and the mandatory power, Great Britain, has also the duty, conformably to the general terms of the mandate, to build up in Palestine a Jewish national home. The recent stubborn trouble between Jew and Arab in Palestine has made the complexity of this problem familiar to the whole world. It is almost certain that if the population of Palestine alone were to be considered, or even a moderate increase in it, the problem would be easily soluble. It is already plain that the economic capacity of Palestine is greater than was once thought, and the Jews have shown what can be done. But we have not only to think of a group of Arabs and a group of Jews domiciled in Palestine, but of two world forces, Jewry and Islam, to each of which Palestine is a holy land. Zionism through the mouths of its wilder leaders desires not a national home in Palestine, but Palestine as a national home. The Arabs have never accepted the idea of the Jewish home, and claim that promises were made to them during the war that have not been fulfilled. Moslems outside Palestine watch with keen interest what goes on in the country, and the burial of Mahomed Ali, the Indian Moslem leader at the Round Table Conference, within the area of the mosque in Jerusalem, was a sign of the interest of world Islam.

One hopeful feature is the excellent quality of the German Jews who have entered Palestine in flight from the nazi policy of modern Germany. They are not Zionists ; indeed—to quote a jest that is going the rounds—the new immigrant is asked, " Do you come from conviction or from Germany ? " But they are tolerant and civilized persons, accustomed to working with Christians, and their influence, though not yet numerically great, is exerted in the interests of concord and understanding.

There is a far better opportunity for the Christian school in Palestine than in any other part of the Near East. Under the mandate there is complete religious freedom. (I may here note that in Palestine there exists a simple and admirable system for registering conversion of every kind.) There is therefore the chance to develop really strong Christian schools in which a worthy policy of Christian education can be carried out. I had the good fortune to be present at a conference of teachers at which almost all the varied groups of Christians in Palestine were represented, and I have never attended any meeting of Christian educators anywhere in the East that seemed more full of ideas and of hope. The Christian schools are, of course, open to all communities, and are able to perform an invaluable ministry of reconciliation. It is pleasant to be able to say this, when it is unfortunately true that the Christian church has somewhat signally failed to offer any reconciling ministry between Jew and Arab, being almost entirely Arab in sympathy, through racial ties.

I think that what has been said in this chapter, sketchy as it necessarily has to be, will show how great are the difficulties that confront the work of Christian evangelism in the Near East. I have no space to write of Iraq or Arabia or north Africa. I might add one bit of testimony from Syria. In 1935 the representative of the French mandatory power, answering a question about religious freedom at the meeting of the Permanent Mandates Commission, frankly stated that the administration preferred not to expose converts to the risk of murder by pressing for toleration. The difficulties proceeding from the Moslem church-state idea are plain. In so far as they are being replaced by other difficulties arising from intense nationalism, it can hardly be held that the situation is eased. Nationalism may be a releasing of new energy and power, and when that is the case there is some preparation for the Christian message of freedom and release. But it may be a tyrannical organization of life around some myth of race or blood ; it is incalculable ; it may have nothing whatever to do with freedom. A great authority has commented upon the fact that the mandates commission had to deal with such questions as that of the Assyrians in Iraq at a time " when the totalitarian national state was taking the place of the multi-national empire as the standard form of parochial political organization. The Assyrians in Iraq were the victims of the same turn of the political wheel as the Germans in Poland or the Jews in Germany—and from the humanitarian standpoint the change was not for the better, for the subject nationalities of the old regime had not been faced with that prospect of the total suppression of their national individuality which was the prospective doom, under the new regime, of the alien minorities." [5]

Before we close this survey there are some things that must be said about the life of the church itself in these lands of the Near East. There is a certain stirring within the ancient churches. Societies are being formed within them, such as the Zoë movement in Greece and a similar one in Rumania, for the stimulation of vital religion. Preaching centers are being opened in the villages around Cairo, and though these were intended primarily for arousing the Copts it is frequently the case that Moslems also attend the meetings—a wholly admirable development, and one that perhaps points the way to the future of evangelization in Egypt. At present a convert is nearly always rooted out of his environment

[5] Professor A. J. Toynbee, *Survey of International Affairs*, 1934, p. 114.

and has no society ready naturally to receive him. It is surely plain that the ancient churches, that have during so many centuries kept the faith and resisted intense persecution, have now, with all their backwardness, a great part to play in the evangelization of Islam.

The membership of the Protestant churches has mainly (though there are exceptions, as we have seen) been drawn from the ranks of the older churches, and while this was done with the object of building up a strongly aggressive and evangelistic Christianity, it has aroused intense jealousy and feeling among the ancient churches and has not, on the whole, produced Protestant churches that are markedly different from the older bodies in their attitude to Moslems. Moreover, the tone of Christian thought and life in these countries has been to a large extent set by Islam. It was said to me by several of the most experienced missionaries in the whole region that one of their greatest tasks was to awaken in the church a more Christian idea of God, and to withstand the insistence on dogmatic orthodoxy and outward observance to the neglect of the inner life of religion.

But the greatest difficulty of all is just that there is not enough love for the Moslem on the part of the Christian. This is intelligible enough—there are centuries of history behind it. The Moslem has been and is the ruler ; he judges Christianity by the products of the harried and downtrodden ancient churches ; he is contemptuous. The Christian for his part has often learned subservience ; his experience of converts from Islam has often been unfortunate ; he does not much believe in the conversion of Islam. The small number and the uprooting of the converts makes it hard for them to grow, and so we have something of a vicious circle.

It is a matter for much thankfulness, therefore, that in spite of all these innumerable obstacles there is today more concern for the evangelization of Islam among Christians in the Near East, and more prayer for it, than there has been for many years past. Both among the evangelical churches and the ancient communions and among the missionaries there is the stirring of new hope. It is felt that the Moslems have somehow or other been given a wholly wrong notion of what Christianity is, and that there must be reasons for this which can be discovered so that new ways may be followed. It may be, perhaps, that along with a new and well based evangelistic movement will go new ways of service. The Near East has been distinguished for the great missionary colleges of American foundation. Some of these still do great work, others find the new restrictions crushing. But the changing economic needs of the people both in the rural areas and in the towns may yet reveal ways of constructive service which will enable Christians to show to those who have so much ground for prejudice against them that there is in their hearts nothing but love for the Moslem, and that the offer of the gospel is not a piece of imperialism or diplomacy, nor merely an expression of dogmatic fidelity, but the offer of what is most precious in life.

PART II

REFLECTIONS

V

THE GOSPEL AND THE NEW AGE

THE picture which I have tried to draw in the preceding pages is, I hope, reasonably objective. Any statement of a situation is bound to be colored by the convictions of the person who makes it, because it is from that source that all judgments of value must necessarily come. But I have tried to let the facts as I saw them speak to me, and not to insist on seeing only such facts as suited my book. Out of that broad sketch two things stand out conspicuously. The first is the increasing menace and difficulty that surround and threaten the whole Christian enterprise and the very existence of the Christian church, as a body pledged by the terms of its foundation to spread its message to all mankind. The second is the steady growth and deepening of the evangelistic spirit in the church, and the widening range of success (I use that word in a religious sense) with which the preaching of the gospel is meeting.

One has the feeling of living in a time when great opposing forces are coming to a life-and-death struggle, Berdyaev writes of "the end of our time." There is widely spread the conviction that the cultural tradition which began with the Renaissance, and whose dominant note has been the autonomy of the individual, is coming to an end, and that something new is being born. That same cultural tradition has, as we have seen, powerfully influenced the thinking East. It will pass away there more slowly, just because it is derivative ; to take but one instance, there is, I sometimes think, more talk about democracy in the East than in the West today. But already we can see how each of the two great rival ideas that in the West have supplanted in so many minds the older notions of liberty and the individual is establishing itself in the East—nationalism or fascism or racialism on the one hand, and communism on the other.

To many minds in the West it is now axiomatic that there is to be a struggle between these two rival creeds, as truly a religious war as any in the past, as ruthless and terrible as the Thirty Years' War and far more widely spread in its devastation. Spain today is the scene of just such a struggle, and as I write it is impossible to be sure that the flame will not spread to the rest of Europe. The democracies of Britain, France and America are not confronted with so simple a choice, and may well hold that they know and will maintain a better way. Yet they must recognize the passion that possesses the devotees of the other creeds and the absoluteness of the claims they make. The tolerant spirit of democracy is scarcely enough to counter their absolutisms. There is need of a truer vision, a deeper devotion, a sacrificial spirit still more unreserved. A Christian who ponders over these things will see not only these secular signs of menace and of the ruin that follows upon the clash of irreconcilable hates, but the proof in the world's life of the redeeming activity of a loving God. Is there a Christian way ?

It is utterly useless for any of us to speak about Christianity today unless we mean something as great as this. It is vital to the world situation that it is today the scene of *religious* struggle. I shall write separately of those problems which inhere in the interrelation of the church with the state and the community, but I must here note that there are in the two creeds referred to above some of the marks of religion. Both communism and racial nationalism are religious in these two supremely important respects : first, that they claim the whole man for their service and embrace within their scope the whole of life ; and second, that they are absolute in that they do not seek to justify their claims by reference to any other standard—for instance, the principles of reason—but are *in themselves* of absolute worth and speak as such to their followers.

This is the connection in which we in the West have to speak of Christianity. It is the same in the East, with this difference—that there the background to the characteristically modern struggle is supplied by the ancient non-Christian religions, while in the West the former unification of life was supplied by the Christian system. But in the East Christianity is weak, relatively young, associated with foreign adventure or rule, and even today acknowledged by perhaps only one per cent of the masses of Asia. It is in Buddhism or Hinduism or Islam that the countries of which I have been writing have found in past years the unification of life. Hinduism, for instance, was never merely a religion in the sense that it offered a private consolation to the individual soul ; it was the inspiration of a social order. So with Islam and so with Buddhism. But those days are passing, and for the educated classes and those who through the power of the industrial revolution have been brought within the orbit of the Western culture, I do not believe that the old religions have holding and life-giving power.

What then of Christianity ? I recall a remark made to me by a shrewd Indian Christian who had visited China. He said that three big things had come from the West to China. The first was science ; the second was communism ; the third was Christianity, but it was so vague that everyone seemed to understand it in a different sense. There is some truth in this, not only with regard to China. Those of us who believe that the religion of which Jesus Christ is the center holds the key to all the problems of life and thought must not blind ourselves to the fact that under its name are preached the most diverse beliefs. An infallible church ; an infallible Book ; a moral ideal for human conduct ; an other-worldly pietism ; a social and international program ; a pure pacifism ; the consecration of force ; the corporative state ; the communist state—I might multiply endlessly the opposites which are today preached by reputable Christians as things necessary to or proceeding from the understanding of the Christian religion.

Then there is all the controversy that gathers round the central figure. Perhaps this is now resulting in a certain increase of definiteness and clarity. At least it is plain that the naïve idea that you could drop the Epistles overboard and rest your historical sense securely on a teaching ministry extracted from the Synoptic Gospels, has to be abandoned even by those who most dislike St. Paul, for the new criticism shows that a doctrine of a divine redeeming savior is at the back of the Synoptics. Again, the struggle between those who held that nothing mattered in Christ's teaching except the eschatology (the teaching about the last things) and those who held that it was no true part of his teaching at all, seems to be settling itself, and it begins to be plain that our Lord preached not the coming of a future kingdom but *that the kingdom had come.*

Dr. C. H. Dodd has recently drawn attention, in a small book [1] of high importance, to the fact that there is a clear distinction drawn in the New Testament between the " preaching " and the " teaching." (The Greek words are respectively *kerygma* and *didaché*.) The former was what was set before the non-Christian world. It was Christianity presented as news. It was the cutting edge of the gospel. The latter followed upon it. It comprised instruction in the life of Christ and his teaching, in Christian morals and a host of other things. But first came the preaching. I think that this distinction is of the highest importance for the missionary planning of the church.

What came into the " preaching " ? If we look at the Acts of the Apostles it is not difficult to see in the sermons of St. Peter and others in the early chapters, backed up by the much more copious material later obtainable from St. Paul, what were the main things that were " preached." Here are some central phrases :

[1] *The Apostolic Preaching and its Developments* (Willett, Clark).

The God of our fathers raised up Jesus, whom ye slew, hanging him on a tree. Him did God exalt with his right hand to be a prince and a savior, for to give repentance to Israel, and remission of sins. And we are witnesses of these things ; and so is the Holy Ghost, whom God hath given to them that obey him [Acts 5:30–32].

Him being delivered up by the determinate counsel and foreknowledge of God, ye by the hands of lawless men did crucify and slay ; whom God raised up, having loosed the pangs of death : . . . whereof we all are witnesses. Being therefore by the right hand of God exalted, and having received of the Father the promise of the Holy Ghost, he hath poured forth this, which ye see and hear [Acts 2:23–24, 32–33].

Be baptized every one of you into the name of Jesus Christ unto the remission of your sins ; and ye shall receive the gift of the Holy Ghost [Acts 2:38].

The things which God foreshowed by the mouth of all the prophets, that his Christ should suffer, he thus fulfilled. Repent ye therefore, and turn again, that your sins may be blotted out, that so there may come seasons of refreshing from the presence of the Lord ; and that he may send the Christ who hath been appointed for you, even Jesus [Acts 3:18–20].

Jesus of Nazareth, how that God anointed him with the Holy Ghost and with power ; who went about doing good, and healing all that were oppressed of the devil ; for God was with him. And we are witnesses of all things which he did . . . whom also they slew hanging him upon a tree. Him God raised up the third day, and gave him to

be made manifest . . . unto witnesses that were
chosen before of God, even to us, who did eat and
drink with him after he rose from the dead.   And
he charged us to preach unto the people, and to
testify that this is he which is ordained of God to be
the judge of quick and dead.   To him bear all the
prophets witness, that through his name every one
that believeth on him shall receive remission of
sins [Acts 10:38–43].

I do not think it can be denied that there was a
definite conviction in the minds of those who spoke
in this way that they were not urging upon their
hearers the acceptance of an ideal, but announcing
to them that something of eternal significance and
value *had happened*.   Their preaching was, in a
sense, narration, and all Christian witness is in a
measure narration.   It is the telling of what has happened.

The preaching, then, was to this effect.   God had
revealed to his people that he had a purpose for them,
by his long schooling of the Jews.   In the course of
that preparation he had led them to look for one who
as the chosen of the Father should suffer for men's
sins.   This expectation was fulfilled in Jesus of Nazareth, who was put to death on the cross after showing
by his works of love and his victory over the power of
the devil that the life of the new age was in him.   He
was raised from the dead, showing thus that death
and sin were vanquished and that a new power had
entered into human affairs.   For those who should
believe in him and his atoning death there was remission of sins.   He had received from the Father
the power of the Spirit, and this power was shed upon

those who believed in him and in the community of believers, so that a new creation had come to be. The whole order of history was to find its meaning in these events, and would be ended in a universal judgment by Christ for the Father.

The pages of the New Testament show how fully the task of teaching, as distinct from the preaching of the fundamental news, was undertaken. The memoirs of the life and death and resurrection of the Lord were compiled, and all the difficult ethical problems that had to be faced in the early church were discussed and weighty advice recorded. But beneath it all lay that which was first presented to those without the Word, the news of the redeeming act of God in Christ.

It is, first, a doctrine of *the living God working in history*. Here lies one of the profound differences between biblical religion and all other. There is no other religious tradition in the world in which so continuous insistence is laid upon the working of God in history. For both Hinduism and Buddhism, with all the varieties of sect and school that distinguish them, it is true that the world of historical events is an unreal world. Even the great chain of cause and effect represented by the Hindu law of karma is not *real* in the sense that Brahma is real ; while for the Buddhist the action of karma is due in the last resort only to the existence of desire, and will cease when that is eliminated. The life of the good man in either tradition is not to be spent in doing good so much as in perfecting release and escaping from the personal world of unreality. Even the Confucian tradition, with all its practical emphasis on the human and social virtues, speaks of thousands and thousands of years through which the human cycle rolls, only to return upon itself. The Stoics, who were of great influence among educated people in the time of our Lord, held to the doctrine of endless recurrence; the great wheel of history turned round and round and came back full circle to where it began—but no fruit was garnered and there was no meaning in the process. Dr. Edwyn Bevan suggests [2] that it may have been an element in the success of the gospel preaching that to a generation weary of the futility of things the Christians preached that history was real, because God worked in it his eternal purpose.

That the living God works in history was the core of the prophetic message. The historical books of the Old Testament are not mere annals; they contain the record of the judgment and mercy of God as the writers, influenced by the prophets, saw the history of the chosen people in the light of prophetic truth. In the clash of the great powers of the old days—Egypt, Assyria and Babylon—and the relations of the Jewish nation with them, the prophets saw the judgment of God. If they wished to recall to mind the power and might of God they would make mention of his mighty works, how that he had brought the people up from Egypt, and turned again the captivity of Zion.

What links the Jewish tradition together throughout the checkered history of the nation is the vision of a purpose of God being worked out in the events of history, and the hope of a final fulfillment. That

[2] *Christianity*, pp. 35–36.

fulfillment is in the coming of Christ, who is therefore only truly to be apprehended as coming " in the
fullness of the times." The temporal process, already
known as the vehicle of divine action, will be brought
to a close in judgment, for if history is the record
not of aimless chance but of divine action that action
and purpose must have an end.

I have called this a doctrine of the *living* God, and
the word is all-important. It makes literally all the
difference in the world whether we believe in a God
who is only the result achieved by our thinking, the
postulate of our moral action, or in One who is living, who is before us, before our thought and before
our action, who plans and acts and chooses, whose is
the great initiative, who is the creator, redeemer and
judge. Before such a God the human question is
not, " Can I believe in God ? " but " What wouldst
Thou have me to do ? " This is what is meant in the
difficult and yet luminous language of Karl Barth
when he says that God is not " object " but " subject." We deal with the Living One, not with one
whom, though we may concede that he lives, we treat
only as one called in by our need or accredited by our
thought.

The doctrine, in the second place, is a *doctrine of
God made man*. All the preparation of history and
all the manifold workings of God come to a head in
one supreme event. The Word that was in the beginning with God took flesh. Only so, in a profound
simplicity, could the loving purpose of God be fully
known. But it is not a doctrine of incarnation as so
much of the world has known incarnation—a the-
ophany, a miraculous portent without reference to

the complex web of history, still less a mere facet of the divine side by side with many other incarnations. The church clung to the history of Jesus of Nazareth. Pontius Pilate got into the Apostles' Creed as a bit of contemporary history. Born of woman, born under the law, Jesus of Nazareth lived a human life at a definite point in space and time, within the bounds of our mortality. Nor was it a sham humanity, as of a demigod in the heathen mythologies, walking the earth masked in human form. He was hungry, he was disappointed, he knew what it was to be deserted by his friends, he faced the power of the mob, he loved little children, he rejoiced in the gladness of fellowship. But in this true manhood he showed himself to be in heart and mind and will utterly united with the Father, so that he spoke to men not out of the spiritual learning of the saint but out of an inner authority. In him were released, not for show or to prove a point, but in divine compassion on human need, the divine power over disease and the powers of evil.

When the disciples came to find words for what he was they groped among the vocabularies of the time. He was a prince, a savior, a pioneer of life. But they were always sure of two things, which found expression later in the philosophical language of the creeds : He was truly man ; and he was truly God. Nothing can go beyond what St. Paul says in the Epistle to the Colossians (1:15–17), that Christ is the image of the invisible God, that in him creation finds its meaning, and that in him the whole established order holds together.

Christian thought has never been unaware that in

holding thus firmly to a doctrine which resolutely finds the eternal in time and the universal in one particular, it was embracing as an age-long possession a profound metaphysical difficulty. The Christian doctrine is not of life, light and love ; it is of God becoming man for our salvation. It is not for me here to argue this position, but I would add that all the most vigorous periods in the church's intellectual life are those in which she has most faithfully held to the double truth of an event in time supremely and uniquely indicative of eternal reality. It was always easy to slip to either side, to offer a Greek view of the eternal qualities of God, serene above history, or a picture of a heroic and inspiring character, greater than Socrates or the Buddha, but not the redeemer of the world.

Redeemer—that is the third point. It is a *doctrine of forgiveness and saving from sin*. By redemption I mean in the most definite sense a radical dealing with sin, in the past, in the present and in the future. This is no place to enter into argument over different theories of the atonement. Let us rather recall what happened. We have first the hints that are thrown out in the Old Testament of one who should be numbered with the transgressors though he had done no violence, of whom it could be said that he bore the sin of many, and that by his stripes we are healed. Our Lord himself had much in mind the book in which the most famous of these prophecies are set down. Interwoven with his parabolic teaching and his miracles and works of mercy we find mysterious sayings that point not only to a death voluntarily embraced but to the sense that it had to do with the sins of men and the ransom of many. We move with the gospel record through the earlier time, when his preaching was almost popular, to the turning of the crowd against him and the gathering of the clouds of enmity above his head. In every word and deed he enforces on us the conviction that in him there is a unique and unshared relationship with the Father, and we begin to gain some faint, remote glimpse of what it might mean that one should enter into and bear upon his own self the sins of men—what, it may be, St. Paul meant, in the most mysterious of all his words, when he says of Christ that " he was made to be sin for us " (II Cor. 5:21) . Never is there the note of the empty though splendid tragedy, of the hero whose faithfulness leaves us asking, " To what end this waste ? " Always it is a conscious acceptance of the Father's will ; here supremely he is about his Father's business ; here, in the showing of perfect obedience and perfect love, he is releasing the powers of a new age. The earliest preaching speaks of " remission of sins," and whatever later ages may have made of it no one can read the New Testament and not hear something of the sound of joy and release into new life and power that sings through the pages. Through the love and passion and death of Jesus they had become certain of the forgiveness of God ; Jesus had done for them what they could not have done for themselves ; the old fetters had been broken and a new power had come into life. The cross is linked always with the resurrection—again, never the exaltation of a mere portent, as if the truth received validity because a dead body had been reanimated. It is a double manifestation of the loving power and

counsel of God ; first in the life and death of the beloved, in which God is found to be drawing men to
himself and reconciling them to him, and then in the
triumphant manifestation of the divine power, a
power of which *the ordinary Christian life* was to be
a continuous expression. The dramas of crucifixion
and resurrection were to be repeated in each be-
liever's life ; he was to die to the old self and to rise
in the power of the new age, and it was to be no
vague power that moved him, but the spirit of Jesus.

Let us note, moreover, two things of crucial importance here. First, it is God who initiates, not
man. The world is full of the self-mortifications of
those who have tried (and are at this hour trying in
innumerable places of pilgrimage and sacrifice all
over the world) to get right with God and rid themselves of the burden of sin by their own effort and
offering and agony. Here it is God in Christ that
draws men to himself.

The other consideration is the tremendous effect
which this doctrine, if believed, must have upon our
thought of man. If man is, as St. Paul saw once and
for all, not primarily Jew or Greek, white or colored,
learned or ignorant, rich or poor, proletarian or
bourgeois—not any of these things, but " my brother
for whom Christ died," then a great deal of the
world's policies stands immediately condemned.

Fourth, it is *a doctrine of society*. Nothing is more
remote from the New Testament teaching than the
idea that religion is a matter of private consolation,
without bearing upon the actual world in which we
live. Right back to Abraham and all through the
prophets there is the idea of the divine society, the

remnant, the suffering community, the ideal congregation. The church is the divine society in which the Spirit dwells. The individual Christian lives in the Spirit, but it is a life lived in fellowship, and the fellowship is not that of the club, based upon human likes and dislikes, but is drawn from the gift and life of Christ himself.

This church, this body of Christ, though not *of* the world is still very much *in* the world. It is remote from the Christian spirit to think of the church as withdrawing from the world into a unity of its own. The redeemed life which it manifests is the restoration of that which was ordained in creation ; it is not alien to the world, however much the world may think so ; it is the true way of living. If the church is the token and earnest of the kingdom, that final consummation of all things, it is to witness to the life of the kingdom in the life of the world. It is to resist in the name of Christ all that is contrary to the spirit of Christ, not treating the world as if it had no right and wrong within it, but equally withstanding the notion that men can invent a human society so good and well adjusted that it shall no longer need to be redeemed.

Christians therefore from the earliest times until now have found themselves to be citizens of two kingdoms, or rather, as the writer to the Hebrews puts it, dwellers in one country and yet seekers after another. There is a tension in all real Christian discipleship between that which is and that which should be, between our duty to the established order of things and our witness to the better order which can come only as men have faith and will believe.

Last, it is *a doctrine of man*. Perhaps it is here, even more than in what they think about God, that modern men differ most from one another. What is man ? asked the psalmist ; and we are told today, variously, that he is what his blood and race are ; that he is what his nation is ; that he is the resultant of an economic process and interplay of forces ; that he is the lord of the world. I know of no view other than the Christian that deals realistically with man and with the truth of his complex nature. The Christian faith knows nothing of man as alone by himself in the world ; it knows of man in relation to God and to his fellow man. It sees him held in a perpetual contradiction : a contradiction between the image in which he was made, the image of God, and that corrupted nature which sin has made of him. Surely, as a matter of plain experience, both things are true—the divine image and the marring of it ? But the Christian faith goes on with a third assertion, that the lost or marred image can be restored by Christ.

The secret of living, then, is to die to self, which means among other things to desert the whole range of ideas associated with the autonomy of man and his inherent worth and dignity, and to yield to the truth that life is a matter of persons living together, finding the will and the call of God in the demands which they make on one another, and allowing the spirit of Christ, which is not that of discord or aloofness, but of love, joy, peace, to re-create from within.

There are two marks that always appeal to me as peculiarly eloquent of the Christian spirit in the sphere of action. One is the exhibition of certain virtues that are hardly even within the scope of the standard cardinal virtues, and seem rather silly and even wrong to the just and worldly mind. I mean such things as loving your enemies, going the second mile, turning the other cheek—all those difficult things, so difficult to any of us who take our ethical ideals merely from the better standards of the life around us. For these are the direct fruits of the spirit of Jesus. The foolishness in these acts, the irrationality, is of the same order as his who, when we were yet sinners, died for the ungodly.

The other is that spirit of infinite debt that seems to color and inspire the fullest Christian discipleship. If you turn to the Jesuits, faithful under the tortures of the Indians in Canada, or to William Carey amid his astounding labors in Serampore, or to the Wesleys, or to any saint of any Christian breed, you always find the same thing, whatever differences may coexist. It is the sense that the debt that the Christian soul owes to God in Christ is so great, so infinite, so beyond speech or telling, that nothing save a wholly surrendered life can be offered, and that even such a life is in no way a payment for what has been done. *Pro tanto quid retribuamus?* This is the secret of the passionate service, joyful, unresting, and without a trace of self-regard, which is typical of the Christian life at its noblest.

But here we have come back to where we began. This spirit that works out in service and in life, what is it but the result of the actual impact of the historic Lord Jesus upon the world of men? It is all a part of that which happened when the Son of God became man and the Father " bowed down to bless us in the Son." [3]

[3] A phrase of the late Prof. H. R. Mackintosh in *The Person of Jesus Christ*.

V I

CHURCH, COMMUNITY AND STATE

I APOLOGIZE to the organizers of the conference
to be held by the Universal Christian Council of
Life and Work at Oxford, in July 1937, for borrow-
ing the title of their meeting. I had thought of call-
ing this chapter " Church and Caesar," but it is not
only Caesar that concerns us. When we come to
think over the problems of the Christian church in
the face of the vast and difficult situation sketched in
the earlier part of this book, and to relate to them
the fundamental gospel, nothing presents itself as
more urgent and complex than the connection of the
church not only with the state but with that more
nebulous but also more living and in the last resort
more powerful thing, the community.

This is not a problem of either East or West alone,
but emphatically a world problem. There are, naturally enough, great differences among the countries
and between East and West, broadly speaking, in the
manner in which the question arises. The details are
different, and the background of the past is different.
But there are certain great facts that are common.
There is, first, the authority normally exercised by
the group—Roman or Mogul empire, or city-state in
Greece, or village community anywhere in Asia—

over the life and actions of those who dwell within it. There is, in the second place, the disintegration of these old ideas by the rise in the West of the conception of individual right and freedom, and the transmission of this conception to the East through literature, travel, education and other channels. There is, third, in these latter years the development of the ancient group authority into something more tyrannical than the old world knew, through the influence of a philosophy of the state. This is fundamentally the same whether the authoritative community is dominated by race or nationalism or by the economic vision of the communists. The newspapers are full of the evidences of these tendencies in the European world ; the tendencies are not less plain in the countries of the Near, Middle and Far East. But there is this great difference—that in the West the social and cultural background is impregnated with Christianity, and the church, even in such a country as Russia is today, remains a large and massive organization ; in the East the background is Buddhist, Hindu, Shintoist, Confucian or Moslem, and the church in all its branches taken together is but a tiny thing.

We have seen in some detail what the questions are. In Japan there is the rise of an authoritarian state, using the ancient religious veneration of the emperor as the means to an absolute state authority. This offers immediate dangers to the church, and those dangers have become more evident in Korea and Manchuria than in Japan, because it is in the outlying empire that the new theories are most strongly pressed. We have reflected also that if the

Japanese authority should have its way in China there is reason to fear for the Chinese church, both because it is a church and therefore cannot disobey God, and also because being intimately linked with world Christianity it offers a barrier to an introverted nationalism.

In the Near East we have watched the engrossing struggle between the diametrically opposite conceptions of the Moslem church-state and the rising nationalisms of the Near East countries ; but we have also noted that the new nationalism is not necessarily more tolerant of the Christian church than is the church-state of Moslem history.

We have seen, moreover, that within Japan and China, and in a less though increasing measure in India, there are arising the communist passion and loyalty. This rise is created partly by propaganda from without but still more by the intolerable conditions under which hundreds of millions of people have to live. Perhaps because it is not rooted in the great natural heritages of race and nation but springs from the class organization of industrialism and looks to a future in which the ancient groupings are transcended by a class victory extending across the nations, communism is likely to be more tyrannical and more intolerant even than the mythologies of blood and race. These two great movements of nationalism and communism are, as we have seen, religious. They claim inherent and absolute authority ; they claim the whole man ; men and women are prepared to die for them.

But there is another range of problems before us also as we contemplate the Christian church in Asia.

Not only the state but the community has to be kept in mind. It is a great handicap to the church in almost every land that having been brought from without, often by the agency of Europeans or Americans, it is still foreign in aspect. Sometimes it even carries with it the air of sharing the superiority which the foreign power, political or economic, may enjoy. This is a matter of first importance for, as we shall see, it is not merely desirable on grounds of efficiency and convenience that the church breathe the same air as the community and be in solidarity with it ; it is deeply necessary and right.

It may be only a special case of the question just mentioned, but the relation of an indigenous church to the foreign imperial power ruling a country is often a crucial matter. We find something of this problem all over the East. Sovereign Japan does not know it within her own bounds, but there are signs already that Japanese Christian expansion, accompanying that of the nation, may find itself faced by something of the same difficulties as the Christians of other expanding states have found. In China, though there was little political control, there was so large diplomatic and economic influence exercised by the foreign powers that the revolution was in one aspect a movement to free the country from foreign shackles, and the charge that the Chinese Christians were " running dogs " of the foreign imperialists is familiar. In the Netherlands Indies, where the state has been more openly committed to the propagation of the Christian religion than in any other part of the modern world, the difficulty takes the form that the church has little church-sense and is apt to be regarded and to regard itself as a branch of the state. As the vigor of Javanese nationalism develops, the charge that Christianity is an aspect of Dutch domination will certainly prove an obstacle to the growth of the church. In India it is well known that the difficulty is old and widely felt. In spite of the fact that a rigid neutrality in religion has been maintained by the British government in India, and that a number of British officials, in the picturesque American phrase, "lean over backwards" in their effort to maintain the desired impartiality, the notion is still widespread that Christianity is a part of the raj, and to the younger nationalist-minded Indians it may make the difference between private acceptance of the claim of Christ and outward profession.

It is necessary also to note that though on the whole the Christian forces in the East are small, they are much stronger in some places than in others, and comprise very different types. The contrast is great, for example, between the urban, middle class educated Christians of Japan, less than one per cent of the population, and the Syrian Christians of Travancore who number about a quarter of the population ; or again, the relation of the church to the community is different in the case of the Bataks with their solid block of half a million Christians in the middle of Sumatra or the 85 per cent of Christians in the south of Celebes, from that of the little communities of Christians in the Near East. If there should be a great ingathering of untouchables to the church in India, obviously the whole community would be profoundly affected.

What are the first principles ? What do we mean

by the church ? We must be clear about its fundamental nature. It is the body of Christ, the community of those who are united in common faith, common love and common worship to him who is its life and its head, bound in loyalty to him, inspired by his spirit. Within the church the authority of Christ as king transcends all other loyalties.

It is, further, the community of those who live by the divine miracle of the remission of sins. It is not a society of athletes in moral achievement, but a community of those who, because they are the children of salvation and of divine grace, are born to a new life which impels them toward strenuous moral effort in the spirit of deepest humility.[1]

Again, continuing the prophetic idea of the chosen people, it is a community of " the elect." This does not mean a community of prigs who think themselves better than others, but of those who recognize that in the deepest things it is God's call that matters and not man's choice.

But it is not a community *in vacuo*. It lives in the world, and this carries with it two implications. The first is that it shares in the imperfections of all human things. It is made up of those who are " being saved." It is tainted with human sin and shortcoming. It must always be reaching out in penitence and faith toward the sources of the renewal of its life. As an institution (or, in our distressful condition, a series of institutions) it is subject to the evils that beset all institutions—self-regard, cowardice and sloth. The second implication is that its unity is not to be

[1] I take these sentences, as well as some ideas, from a paper by Dr. H. Kraemer of Java.

thought of as something apart from the common family of mankind. Man was made by God of one blood, and the divisions that sunder humanity are not, as we so often think, more fundamental than the unity to which love calls us. The church, in that common faith and life which even its divisions cannot wholly obscure, points all mankind to the recovery of a lost fellowship which God intends for his children.

How does this guide us when we think of the relation of the church to the community? Surely it leads us to the conviction that the church should be in spirit and life as close to the community as it can be. This is not a matter of expediency but of truth. For the church looks to a God who is both Creator and Redeemer, and it must view with a reverent regard the works of his creation. Race and blood, language and family and all that belongs to the common fundamental life of man then become a part of God's furnishing of the house of human life. It is not merely politic that the church should be indigenous; apart from a share in the common life of man it can have no life at all.

Hence the immense importance of a strong native leadership in the church. I repeat that this is not a matter of tactics. We are being driven in these days of financial stringency to a larger trust in the indigenous leadership of the younger churches, and sometimes it looks to them as though it were only the economic argument that led the older churches in their missionary activity to this policy. Nothing could be further from the truth. It is not a money argument, nor even merely the recognition that the

Christian people of the land are nearer to their own countrymen and can be evangelists and interpreters of Christ as no foreigner can be. It is an acknowledgment that a church that is faithful to the redeeming God must not forget the works of his creation.

It is therefore a first necessity that the whole planning of the life of the church in these great lands of the East should have in the forefront of policy the need for a truly indigenous leadership, and that in worship, church organization, education and social upbuilding the natural faculties and traditional heritage of the people should be followed. Most of all is this true in the realms of worship and of Christian thought. Because worship is the deepest expression of itself that human nature knows, it is essential that it shall gather into itself everything that each people has to offer to God. Alien forms may have their place in the infancy of the church when there is no other alternative, but their permanence (except when as in some of the simplest and profoundest elements in Christian worship they become native to every soil) can only make for a stunted life.

Similarly, there is little that is so important in the Christian life of Asia as that there should be raised up a greater number of Christians with an original insight into the meaning of the Christian religion. By original I do not mean that they should hunt for the bizarre and the *outré*, still less that they should try, as has sometimes been done, to graft the Christian olive on to the Hindu or Buddhist stem. I mean simply that the church needs those who have seen the truth for themselves and made it their own, able to use the historic treasures of Western Christian thinking without being in bondage to their forms, able also to think out for themselves, in the language and thought forms of their own people, the eternal truths of the gospel.

It follows that the church ought to enter as fully as it can into the service of the community through education, social service and medical work. To express the Christian spirit to the life of the people it must enter as deeply as possible into it. It is, I hope, needless to say that this is not to be done only as a bait for evangelizing. Nothing could be more unchristian. Man's life is a whole, not a piebald mixture of sacred and secular. It is as wrong to regard evangelistic work alone as spiritual as to do educational or social work as though that were the sole aim of the church. The multiplication of active, intelligent, well ordered lives in a healthy community is among the fruits of the Spirit, and service directed to that end is one of the expressions of Christian devotion. It may, indeed, be found that so great misunderstanding exists of the meaning and nature of the church that long years have to be spent in service along one or another avenue of approach to the life of the community before the people come to understand that the Christians desire only their good.

Such service is a recognition of the solidarity of the church with the community. It must, nevertheless, just because it is rendered in the name of Christ, always look beyond the present standards to better ones, in criticism, revision and reconstruction. We have, happily, multitudinous instances of this policy in practice. The rural school and teachers' training institute that unite a deep regard for the life of the village with the best pedagogical knowledge available ; the pioneering education for girls and women ; the large responsibility assumed by Christians for some of the most difficult aspects of physical service, such as the care of lepers, of the tuberculous, of the blind and deaf and dumb ; the widespread adoption by Christian bodies of the method of rural cooperative credit—these are only a few of the ways in which the church is showing itself to be at one with the community while pointing beyond the stage to which the people of the land would unaided give their full assent.

Is it recognized in the West how gigantic are these tasks that face the communities of Asia and Africa in which the Christian church is set ? This book is not written with any knowledge of African problems, but it is right to say here that this matter of the church's aiding in the life of the community is more urgent and difficult in Africa than anywhere else in the world, save perhaps among the islands of the Pacific. Asia and Africa alike are subjected in these years to the tremendous strain of meeting and absorbing the intellectual and economic influences that pour in from the West. It is no mere rhetoric to speak of a revolution. But the older Eastern peoples with their written culture have resisting power that the tribal African has not. It is impossible to maintain the tribal society as it is ; it cannot but be changed, and the supreme question is whether it is to drift into chaos or whether ordered life shall be built up out of it. It is almost universally recognized that in this work the Christian church is indispensable, and on their side anthropologists have brought to the church, whenever it would listen to them, great new resources of wisdom.

It may serve as a transition to the problems offered by the state if we stay for a moment to consider the relation of the church to nationalism, which is the expression of the spirit of the community especially in contact with forces that inhibit and limit it. Broadly, it seems to me that any church ought to be in sympathy with political national aspirations. A certain type of nationalism is a great evil in the modern world, but the evil type is in the main shown by powers in the West which have become intoxicated with race or blood myths. In the East it is as yet only Japan that has the power to be aggressively nationalist as certain European powers are today. The main type of Eastern nationalism is the Indian, sensitively conscious of being subject to another people and striving to attain effective power within its own house, or the Turkish or Iranian, where nationalism is the vehicle of a resurgent national consciousness, invading every part of life and culture. Any Indian church, being made up of Indians, will normally sympathize with the national point of view in regard to constitutional reform and the attainment of freedom. Iranian Christians, as we have seen, including converts from Islam, hold themselves to be not less Iranian because they are Christian.

Yet the same principles hold here as elsewhere. Because for Christians no society, not even the most perfect that we can conceive, ceases to be in need of redemption, they cannot enter blindly into a nationalist movement nor forego the duty of criticizing it in the light of the ideal.

The foreign missionary is in a different position. The concrete situations which arise are so different that it is useless to generalize. A foreign missionary in a country ruled by a foreign power different from his own has to be bound by the necessities of the case, which obviously include an abstinence from open indulgence in political activity. This applies, for example, to British in Korea or to Americans in India. It is perfectly possible to show a sympathy with the objectives of a national movement without overstepping the bounds which are proper to such a case. The foreign missionary whose nationality is the same as that of the dominant power is placed in a rather different situation. The fact that he is of the same people as the rulers will predispose him to agree with them and see things as they see them ; he will therefore have to watch his actions with peculiar care lest he allow his national sympathy to estrange him from the Christians of the land with whom he is working. Because missionaries of other nationalities are precluded from public statement it is the more incumbent upon him not to be silent in the face of gross injustice.

The foreign missionary working in the territory of an Asiatic power which is fully self-governing has no problem at this point, though he has others that are grave enough.

While I suggest that nationalism in itself is a good thing, and that it has brought fresh life to many peoples in art, literature, science, philosophy, religion and many other spheres of activity, we must not allow ourselves to forget that nationalism in the militant form can be as great a tyranny as any in the world. Here the question becomes the same as that of the church in relation to the authoritarian state, and to this we now turn.

We have a double fact to consider in the state, just as we have in the church. On the one hand, it is agreed by Christian thinkers that the authority of the state has a divine sanction, and that it is therefore entitled to the obedience of its subjects, not merely because it can wield overwhelming force against the individual but because that obedience is its due. This does not apply only to a good government (which is, in any case, obviously a matter on which men may differ) and certainly not only to a Christian one. It is worth remembering, as the Archbishop of York reminds us, that St. Paul's " the powers that be are ordained of God " was spoken of Nero ! Obedience to established authority is the normally right attitude for the Christian, whether the authority is Christian or not, and whether he approves of it in all respects or not.

On the other hand, society owes almost as much to the rebel as to the statesman. It would be altogether wrong so far to exalt the principle of normal obedience to established authority as to obscure the place of conscience. This is not the place to attempt even a statement, much less an exposition, of the relation between conscience and the state ; but it may be said in a word that because the principle holds that all human societies need to be redeemed, the Christian man must hold in a kind of tension the obedience he owes to constituted authority and the testimony he must give to the higher order of things.

But it must be conscience (not only his own but his own taught by that of the Christian community) that he obeys, and he must never take the name of God in vain, as he will do if he withstands in the name of Christian faithfulness measures to which his real objection is political or economic, or of some other legitimate but wholly mundane kind. I do not suggest that there is no place for rebellion in the name of other kinds of convictions—far from it ; but if we are thinking of the church in its relation to the state, it is only a profoundly conscientious objection to something which offends the Christian conscience that the church can sustain on Christian grounds.

If we take this stand, we are free from a danger which has sometimes beset the church in its relations with the state. The reason for the church's opposition should never be envy or jealousy of the state, as though it were anxious to preserve its own prestige. Once the church begins to fight with weapons of that kind its hopes are gone. Its ground of action lies in those great truths to which it owes its existence. The gravity of the situation in which the church finds itself today in more than one land lies in the fact that the state is denying the truth about the nature of life and of mankind and trying to impose a false orthodoxy of its own. If it is true, as we have said, that man is essentially one to whom God speaks, the child of God intended to find himself in the world as a fellow with others in doing the will of God, then it is not true that there is no call upon him higher than that of his nation, or that he is the result of the economic interplay of forces, or that he is what his race and blood are and no more. The church needs not to organize opposition on such matters ; its very existence and the fellowship and interior life which it enjoys are hostile to all such subpersonal or merely biological views of man.

Moreover, the church is a universal society.   It should, as we have seen, be a home for all men in every land, but if it ever yields to national pride so much as to lose its sense of the universal Christian fellowship, it has lost its savor.   It is in actual fact one of the outstanding facts about the younger churches in the East today that they are in touch with the rest of the world, and that through missionary connection and such events as the Indian Mission of Fellowship to Great Britain they are coming to feel themselves a part of a world fellowship.   No one could be present at the Jerusalem meeting of the International Missionary Council in 1928 and not realize this fact with an unforgettable vividness.   But this is not what is desired by some of those who in powerful places are trying to remold the thinking of the nations.   A national church—one fully sympathetic to the national viewpoint and appreciative of the national destiny—yes ; but this corrected by a universal fellowship and by actual contact with religious helpers from other nations—emphatically no.

Where does the menace lie and where are difficulties most likely to break out ?   If it is the very existence of the church that is an offence it will be denounced either as unpatriotic (by the absolute racial or national state) or as the peddler of opiate to the people (by the communist absolutism) .   These are extremes, but there are certain concrete difficulties already being met in the spheres of evangelism and of education.

I have written something about the conversion problem as it arises in the Near East. It can hardly be said that at the worst in these countries conversion is prohibited. Its legal recognition is impeded by the Sharia law, and the fact of it is strenuously opposed both by Moslem orthodox sentiment and by (some) nationalism. (I am not here including Arabia or Afghanistan in which, I imagine, conversion openly professed is not possible save on pain of death.) But it is quite possible that in one of a number of states organized converting activity might be prohibited. It has actually been proposed by the editor of the *Indian Social Reformer* of Bombay that proselytism shall be forbidden by law and the king-emperor declared protector of all the religions of India. It cannot in my judgment be deemed absurd to suggest that such measures might be passed in several of the Near East countries, and we live in a world of such incalculable change that the same kind of action might be taken elsewhere. If that happened, it would throw the weight of Christian work more than ever upon the indigenous church. It cannot perhaps be claimed as a Christian necessity that Americans or British shall preach the Christian gospel in Iran, for instance, but it is a Christian duty for Iranian Christians to witness to it in their own way and in their own land. The state can never prevent Christian witness, though it may make it dangerous to the last degree and may surround the act of conversion and baptism with legal penalties (loss of property, marriage difficulties and the like) so grave as to render it nearly impossible.

Christian education is at the moment the type of work most generally endangered by state pressure. This pressure is found even where, as in China, there is genuine friendliness to Christian activity on the part of government. To prohibit the teaching of religion in registered private schools of the elementary grade seems to me to be a real interference with the liberty of the subject, but this is the law in China. In Japan the registered school of every grade is subject to the same disability. The obstacle is surmounted by the use of non-school buildings and organized employment of leisure time, both of which are well within the law. Missionary schools in Turkey and in Iran have been hindered by laws which insist that only nationals of the country shall conduct schools of certain grades. In Korea there is obviously a determination not to permit foreign schools unless they will accept shrine worship, and the ultranationalist policy of Japan must make the future of the Christian school under foreign heads, or employing foreigners, somewhat uncertain. (I was asked in Korea whether the meeting of the International Missionary Council to be held in China in 1938 would consider the question : " What is the substitute for Christian education ? " I think this meant that for some missionaries it had become at least an open question whether Christian education in any real sense of the word could go on. In that case, was there any other form of work that might carry some of the same values ?)

What policy can we follow in such emergencies ?

I believe that there is no short and easy answer to this question, and that in the present era of missionary work there are few questions that so much demand corporate study.   I make two suggestions only. The first is that we should avoid every justifiable occasion of offense, and be studiously careful not to ask for privileges as if they were rights to which conscience compelled us to cling.   By occasions of offense I mean such things as the maintenance of schools that have no real educational value and are in reality preaching stations.   (It is said by those who should know that what lies behind the present Chinese policy is the intention of forcing schools to have a real educational purpose.)   It goes without saying that proselytism in the sense in which our Lord uses the word should be sedulously avoided.   Again, if Christian schools and influence are thought to be denationalizing—a frequent charge—the first thing to be done is to examine ourselves and see how far the allegation is true.   Or again, the old days of the dominance of the West in the East have gone, but it is still difficult for some of us to get rid of the idea that foreign missions should have special privileges. Whether we think it wise or not is beside the point ; it is entirely justifiable for a state to insist on its own rules as to vernacular, or the local government of schools, or the foreign holding of property for missionary purposes.   If necessary it is always possible to remonstrate and urge a wiser course, but there is a difference between this and conscientious objection.

The other line of answer is far more fundamental. In the last resort the only weapon that the Christian church has is its own quality of life, its purity and humility and dependence upon God, the dynamic spiritual power which he gives it. The basic demands of the Christian discipleship are perhaps these : worship, witness, the Christian teaching of children. Legal difficulties may hamper but they can be surmounted if there is the zeal to do so. But it can never be right to give up worship at the call of the state, or to give up witness (though methods may have to change), or to fail to teach one's children what the life in Christ is. And it can never be right to worship false gods, not though all the powers of the state call upon us.

Therefore, the key to the problem of the state and its pressure upon the church is finally to be found in the deepening of the life of the church. It is fatally easy to become so engrossed in the detailed work of securing legal toleration for Christian activity as to lose that dynamic redeeming power which is the final charter of the Christian society in the world. The *ultima ratio* on which the church in all ages has fallen back is martyrdom, and in our day there are more Christians in both East and West who are thinking and talking in these terms than there have been for many generations. But martyrdom is, as the word signifies, witness, and there is no witness except out of the depth of life. There is nothing for which the prayers of the universal church are so greatly needed as that there should be deepened and strengthened in the younger churches, faced by so great difficulties and with so slender resources of their own, the authentic life of the Spirit.

VII

THE LIFE AND WITNESS OF THE CHURCH

WE MUST turn now from this somewhat general consideration of the fundamental ground on which the Christian church stands, and its relation to the world order within which it is set, to the questions which inhere in its own life and witness. In a book of this size it is impossible to argue thoroughly the innumerable points of principle which arise, and I hope that what I have said in the two preceding chapters will make it plain why I do not believe in the permanence or value of a " Christian movement " apart from an enduring Christian society. The Christian religion is concerned not merely with the promulgation of ideals but with a life lived in response to the historic revelation of the eternal God. Everything depends, under God, upon the quality of life manifested by those who have been called together into the fellowship of the church, not by their common disposition but by the miracle of redemption and the obedience which it demands. The church is rooted far back in God's promise to Abraham, but in the long discipline of the chosen people—chosen, unlike the nationally elect of the modern world, in order that they might suffer and by suffering be purified—it has been freed from everything that is local, racial or partisan. To these great standards it can always be recalled.

" Life " and " witness "—the two must go together. Those of us who emphasize the primacy of the church in missionary policy are sometimes told that we exalt the welfare of an institution and forget the manifold diversity of life. But it is obvious that so soon as the church becomes a static and self-regarding society it has to that extent ceased to be the church of Christ. Called into being by the divine love, it has no life apart from its witness to that love. It is in the world, and so long as time shall last it will partake of the infirmity of human things, but it exists to bear witness to the redeeming purpose of God and in a measure to be the vehicle of that purpose.

I have tried in my earlier chapters to paint a picture in which there are not only deep shadows—and they are deep indeed—but also brilliant lights. It is, I believe, the truth of the world situation that faces us as Christians today that there is both increasing menace from the secular order and abundant evidence of the outpouring of the Spirit. The advance of the Christian forces is to be prompted not by the human spirit of bravado, crying " *Toujours l'audace !* " as it assails its foes, but by obedience to the divine leading. It is the plain fact that God is so leading the church, and it is through his working in the hearts of men that there is today throughout the church in these great lands of the East an absorption and commitment to the task of evangelistic witness that has not always been present either in them or in the churches of the West.

Something has been said already of the evangelistic

movements now on foot in India, China and Japan. The " Kingdom of God " movement in Japan came to an end in its organized form, and has now been succeeded by another nation-wide movement in which all the non-Roman churches are united. The earlier movement owed its chief impetus to the genius of Toyohiko Kagawa, and bore the impress of his spirit in its twin emphasis upon personal evangelism and the establishment of cooperative societies [1] as a necessary part of the Christian witness in life. The present movement is more firmly based upon the conscious cooperation of the different Christian bodies ; it is not quite clear how far it is committed to the necessity of Christian action in the social sphere as an essential part of the Christian witness.

In China, the five year movement launched in 1930 has completed its first phase and has been renewed for another five year period. To double the Christian church membership in China was the original objective—though it would be misleading to write as though a severely numerical goal described the aims of such leaders as Dr. Cheng Ching-yi. The movement was carried through at a time when every kind of difficulty faced both nation and church—flood, famine, foreign invasion, internal confusion—and any body of Christians in the world might have been excused had they conceived their duty as being only to " dig themselves in " and wait for kindlier days. In fact, the movement saved the church from the spirit of defeat, and led to deeper life and consecration within its ranks. Of all its features none is more

[1] On the Kagawa cooperatives see Chap. VIII.

interesting to the student from without than the stress laid upon Christianizing the home. In the renewed movement especial attention is being given to the all-important problem of providing adequate Christian training for voluntary lay workers, and to this we shall return.

The Indian churches are faced, as we have seen, with a series of movements, particularly among the depressed classes, which in the coming days will tax to the full all the resources that they can muster. To add another concrete instance to those already quoted, the (English) Methodist Church in Dharapuram, near Coimbatore, has seen a group of Christians which after ninety years of work numbered in the year 1912 just over 2000 and appeared completely stationary, begin suddenly to grow until in 1934 it had reached almost 24,000, though there were actually fewer missionaries in the station in that year than during the twenty years before and an appropriation of barely twice as much money from the mission as at the earlier date. The forward evangelistic movement begun in 1935 by the National Christian Council is not a series of isolated efforts and temporary though spectacular " drives," but a steady advance throughout the mass of the churches, such as alone can meet the innumerable opportunities afforded by India today.

I think it is not too much to say that in all these instances there is one principle universally accepted. It is that the primary instrument of evangelism is *the witness of the church itself*. I do not except the Moslem lands of the Near East, for though the church life in these lands is totally different in its background and conditions from that of the Far East, there is the same recognition as in India, China and Japan that it is on the witness of the church, whether the newer communities of converts or the ancient churches, that the future hangs.

What, in practice, does this mean ?   I can give no better illustration than by quoting the letter of counsel recently sent to the missions and churches of India by the little group who advise the National Christian Council on evangelism.   The salient points of this letter are the primacy of personal witness ; the necessity of showing practical sympathy with the untouchables in their distress and extending a friendly welcome to all who seek the succor of the Christian faith ; the importance of simple united Christian worship from the very beginning as an uplifting and liberating influence ; the need for providing resident Christian teachers where the spirit of inquiry is abroad and giving such instruction as will lead new disciples into a gradual understanding and apprehension of the essential Christian doctrines ; the larger employment of voluntary workers ; the greater use of training schools for inquirers ; the overcoming of illiteracy ; and the practice, above all, of united and continual prayer.

Too much emphasis can hardly be given to the place of worship in the life of the church.   It is among the most interesting and valuable points in Bishop Pickett's survey of mass movement work that he insists upon the value of worship, and of liturgical worship, for the untouchable converts as the most powerful means of teaching them the inner meaning of the Christian religion.   Worship is from the human side the completest exercise of the personality : worship is more than knowledge, though Christian worship must be intelligent worship. The worship of God, deep and simple, is both the life-blood of the young churches that are growing up so rapidly among masses of unlettered people and also a means of witness that is unsurpassed.

Of personal witness by unpaid lay workers of the rank and file there is already a volume that would put to shame almost any Christian body in the West. It was one of the features of the " Kingdom of God " movement in Japan that great numbers of laymen took part. In India the new evangelistic movement is everywhere enlisting the witness of the lay members. In one effort in western India it is said that " all who could sing and walk took part." The Bishop of Dornakal recently reported that in a period of concentration upon evangelistic witness more than half of the communicant membership of the diocese actually engaged in some form of personal evangelism. Young men from the churches in south Travancore spent their holidays in traveling among the Ezhava communities to tell them what they knew of the grace of God. A missionary writing from the midst of the Bhil people, aborigines in central and western India among whom there is a great movement toward Christ, says that it is a characteristic of those who have been converted that they are eager to carry their message among the villages, and that in consequence one of the main problems now facing the mission is " the constantly increasing number of those who have received the gospel in this way from poorly equipped though intensely earnest followers of Christ, and their insistent demands for further and more effective teaching." [2]

This brings us to the question of training and education. It is an immense subject and we can do no more than indicate some of its facets. Clearly, movements of the size now being faced in India and perhaps soon to be faced elsewhere require nothing less than a vast offering of voluntary witness, and it is one of the principal tasks now upon us to provide simple and adequate training for those who will be, to such extent as their condition allows, voluntary workers. The recent study made in China, under the leadership of Dean Weigle of Yale, of the whole provision of training for Christian service in China laid much emphasis upon this problem, and the methods now being followed by the National Christian Council of China in fostering simple and effective religious education among Christians for the purpose of fitting them for this work of witness is of the highest importance, not only to China but to other countries also.

But the greater the army of such workers, the greater the need for the training of the abler leaders. Here we touch the question of theological training, one of the most difficult and important in all missionary work. For reasons that are obvious, the forces of tradition are unusually powerful here, and the theological seminaries and colleges are not always attuned to the urgent needs of the day. Denominational loyalties have resulted in the establishment of too many weakly staffed institutions ; it follows inevitably that they are too often conventionally modeled on a West-

[2] Dr. F. H. Russell in *N.C.C. Review,* July, 1936.

ern pattern, for only the strong staff has the ability and courage to experiment ; they are sometimes slow in adapting themselves to the actual, urgent and changing needs of the times. There are, of course, splendid instances to the contrary, but the strongly marked traditionalism which distinguishes theological education in the West is accentuated in the East by the causes I have mentioned. It is of little use to generalize, but at least we can say that there is need for the best possible training that the Christian world affords to be given to those who are to be the leaders of the younger churches. It is in vain to talk of the " decrease " of the missionary and the " increase " of the indigenous leader unless the best training is given, for responsibility inevitably goes where there is ability to shoulder it. There is no greater need in the Christian life of the East than for an increase in the number of those who have thought deeply upon the meaning of the gospel, have seen its relevance to the historic culture of their peoples, have mastered traditional Christian thinking so that they are not slavishly bound by it but can use it with a true freedom, and are thus enabled to lead in the great work of setting forth the truth among the varied and changing thought forms of the Eastern world. I do not believe that anything like this will be achieved without a considerably greater amount of unified action than is now in sight.

But specifically, religious teaching is only a part of the wider work of Christian education. It is plain, as we look at the circumstances now prevailing in a number of the Eastern countries, that the share to be taken by Christian institutions in general educa-

tion has been reduced and is likely to be further reduced, if not banished altogether in some countries.
I am sure that Christian bodies should cling to a share
in this work as long as they can.   They should, of
course, maintain only schools and colleges which are
of first-rate quality, not merely in academic standing
but in personal influence and in alertness, to meet the
needs of the people.   If the best that can be said of a
Christian school or college is that it is doing the same
sort of thing as schools or colleges conducted by government or private agency, and doing it about as well,
it is at least doubtful whether this is a right use of
man power.   But granted this principle, the case for
taking a share in general education is surely very
strong.   There are many ways of evangelism, and a
good school or college can be among the most effective.   It can show by the strength of corporate life
what the Christian way is.   It can *prepare the mind
for the truth*.   The message of Christianity is to be
interpreted to men and women who are not without
their own preconceptions and convictions and have
been brought up to certain ideas of life which may
be, and often are, in themselves barriers to the gospel.
Not only the specific teaching of Christianity, but the
teaching of science, or literature, or history,[3] can be
used as a preparation for the gospel, because by their
aid wrong views of God and the world can be eradicated and the way made plain—so far as intellectually
it can be made plain—for the truth.

But it will be mainly with Christians, as the years
go on, that Christian education is concerned, and the

---

[3] See *Christian Higher Education in India* (Lindsay report), pp.
148 ff.

need and scope are gigantic. I have written else-where of the importance of abolishing illiteracy, which is within the power of educational agencies if they are properly used and supported. Even within the Christian community there is a great need for the removal of illiteracy, and as the crowds of illiterates pour into the church the need grows ever greater. We are altogether too complacent in this matter. In certain parts of India the proportion of literacy among Christians is actually decreasing, even though no great ingathering of new converts has taken place. Not nearly enough use is being made of the invalu-able insight already obtained into method ; it is hu-miliating to find secular educators sometimes more appreciative of the best Christian pioneering efforts in education than many Christian missionaries.

We need a new spirit of resolution in this matter. Recent years have seen almost every aspect of Chris-tian education in the East examined by able investi-gators—colleges, schools, rural training—but there is too little corresponding zeal in action. In the educa-tion of women and girls and in the field of rural edu-cational experiment the Christian bodies are as truly pioneers today as were Carey and Duff when they began to use the educational method. Too much middle and high school and college education has yielded to the immensely powerful conventionalism of government systems ; a way out can be found and in many cases has been marked out, but only a vigor-ous corporate policy, deeply fraught with a sense of the responsibility of Christian education in the world today, will enable these ways to be chosen.

I do not wish to write unfairly of government and

other available types of school and college ; in India, China and Japan alike it is now true that the best government institutions are academically superior to most of the Christian ones.   (In Japan there is no comparison, for the imperial universities are acknowledged to be on a level of their own.)   But I am convinced that a truly Christian education is something that only Christian educators can give, and that to allow the youth of the growing churches to receive their insights into the meaning of life mainly or only from those who either accept the new paganisms or are uneasily loyal to the old, is to weaken the church of the future and to jeopardize its distinctive Christian witness.

In saying this I do not dispute the fact that the Christian, or at least the missionary, institutions may be driven not only from general education but even from the education of Christians.   I offer this argument not to those who are faced with dire necessity, but to those who think that education is a part of the total labor of the church which may be treated as relatively unimportant.   They are, I believe, tacitly arguing from conditions in the West where there is, to put it at the lowest, a Christian tradition.

But we have been thinking only of evangelistic work and of education.   It is, I hope, plain from all that has been said that there is not one single type of evangelistic work, but a Christian body reaching out in manifold ways to those around, and using every human association as a vehicle of the good news. The changing times in which we live demand a great alertness of spirit in this matter.   Perhaps we have grown too well used to a tripartite division into evangelists, educators and medicals. The evangelist has to use educational methods ; the educator is an evangelist using his own proper instrument ; the physician alone of them all has the power to convey a spirit of love and compassion almost without words, but who can be more of an evangelist than he ? The newer plans for rural reconstruction, to which we shall come later, offer countless ways of making plain what is the message and gift of Christ.

One of the most remarkable of the newer methods is that of newspaper evangelism—the insertion in the ordinary secular press of articles expounding the Christian faith. It was first used in Japan, as is to be expected in a literate country where newspapers have gigantic circulations. In that country the method has been conspicuously successful in arousing interest, which in many cases has led on to definite instruction and conversion. It has now been begun in India and China, and is being used in the Near East through the medium of Turkish and Arabic.

In what has been said in this chapter there has been perhaps a somewhat confused use of the words "missions" and "churches," and it is time to say something on this point. For some of the chief ecclesiastical traditions there is, formally at least, no problem. The Anglican Church organizes dioceses in the Eastern countries and anticipates the gradual disappearance of the mission organization in the field, all the work being controlled by the diocese. This has come to pass in Japan and China to a large extent, and also in parts of India. The Methodist churches of both England and the United States follow a similar principle. It is still possible that within the unified church organization on the field there may be a predominance of missionary influence, but the missionaries are there as members of the church and it is in every case only a question of time before the control is actually in the hands of the Christians of the land.   Other types of organization, however, exist.   The bulk of the Presbyterian, Congregationalist and Baptist missions have side by side a mission and a church, and two main types of policy arise from this fact.   Certain bodies, mainly Congregationalist and Baptist, have virtually merged the mission in the church, leaving perhaps some committee concerned only with the personal affairs of the missionaries. Others, chiefly Presbyterian, have maintained the two bodies in separation but have aimed at passing over control of ever increasing areas of work to the indigenous church, or to committees jointly representative of both church and mission.   The methods in use relate to different types of ecclesiastical organization and need not be discussed here.

What underlies this tangled and somewhat tedious question is the fact that unless there is a satisfactory solution of the relationship of the foreign missionary and the indigenous church leader the maximum of harm can be done to the church and to its life and witness.   It is far from being merely a technical question.   Nothing has more irked the sensitive missionary in every country than to be paymaster of those with whom he must work in the common task, but this stage still has not been passed in, I suppose, the greater number of cases, and cannot be passed unless a certain grade of ability has arisen among the indigenous leaders.   Again, if evangelistic work is initiated by the mission and thought to be the job of the mission, while the church is concerned with the pastoral care of those who are already Christians, a vicious dichotomy is set up ; evangelism is thought to depend upon the amount of money the mission board can spend upon evangelists, and the church, upon whose own witness everything really depends, is thought to have no concern with it. Ideas such as these have been distressingly common and it is only by a wholehearted emphasis upon the true meaning and function of the church that they can be eradicated.

Then there is the whole complex of more personal questions, gathering around the relationships of the workers, indigenous and foreign. So much has been said on this question that I do not wish to write of it at length. But I would make two observations. The first is that the question is a real question, based upon a real difficulty, and that those who make light of it are almost certainly themselves guilty of some of the subtler forms of self-deceit. The missionary movement in the modern world differs radically from the methods whereby the Christian religion was propagated in, let us say, the Roman Empire, in that the initiative has been taken by people from countries totally different in their culture and their economic standards from those to which they went, and, in the case of the predominantly north European and American Protestant missionaries, possessed of a racial habit of initiative and love of creative control. They have, in short, been quite extraordinarily different from those to whom they went. So long as the paternal relationship subsists (and in a good deal of the world it subsists still, and rightly so) the problem hardly arises, though even in fathers good manners are not amiss. But all through the East even where there are masses of illiterate converts there are also leaders of conscious power, and there is a national background impatient of Western self-assertion and political or economic dominance. The modern task confronting the total Christian forces is to be essayed by a kind of double body, so far at least as the greater part of the East and Africa is concerned. The larger partner numerically (and more and more in every other way) must be the church of each land. The other partner is the church, or churches, of the West, working through missionary organizations and represented personally in myriads of intimate contacts by those who are called missionaries. There is the further fact, differentiating the Christian problem from that of colonial governments and the like, that a certain amount of the total money needed is provided by the Western churches. Obviously there is here a situation fraught with difficulty, and it is merely sentimental to pretend that there is none. But the difficulty *must* be surmounted, for unless the total force can advance to its task with the sense of a united life burning within it, it cannot expect to do the work of God in the world. So long as the indigenous worker feels that the real responsibility lies with the foreigner and that he is employed as an agent in a task whose burden lies upon another, he cannot be a witness ; he can be only, what he is still sometimes called, an " agent." Conversely, it is possible for the self-government within the church to go so far that the place of the missionary, though he is in general wanted and valued, is insufficiently clear, and men and women are left wondering just why they came and whether they ought to stay.

The other observation I would offer is that I found much ground to doubt whether we of the West are as far along the road to success in solving this problem as we usually think. I must say candidly that the conditions of the problem are far more difficult in countries still subject in greater or less measure to a foreign power. Japan and China are quite different from India or Java. I confess to being surprised to find how many Indian Christians spoke to me somewhat bitterly on the subject; I had thought that the large advance in devolution of authority to Indian church bodies had largely removed what had been a widely felt grievance. But even after discounting a good deal of personal feeling aroused by untypical cases, I found it impossible to rid myself of the unhappy sense that there was less unity of spirit between the two parties than most of us Europeans and Americans are wont to claim, and in such affairs it is essential that not only oneself should be sure that all is well, but the other man also ! It is right to add that the conditions of a non-self-governing country offer special temptations to those of the same race as the rulers. Most British and American missionaries in India, and most Dutch ones in Java, would find the conditions in Japan a great surprise, as I did. I found myself reflecting that without doubt I had been unconsciously irritating and wounding my Indian friends during the years of my service in India, though I should probably have been annoyed if I had been told so.

This book is not intended to be a general treatise

on missionary work, but there is one problem in this foreign-native connection which I ought to mention, as it is both typical of the difficulties which have to be faced, and is in itself very difficult to decide. One would say that among the first things for which a growing church should be responsible is the support of its own ministry, and that for the foreign sources to provide pastoral care for the local congregations is to prevent them from growing. But, as several Chinese pastors said to me at different times : " You people ask us to do two things which are mutually incompatible. You tell us that the church ought to be led by the best trained ministry obtainable, and you tell us also that we must be self-supporting. We can't manage both." Actually there is, all over the East, a striking and notorious disparity between the salary which a man or woman can expect to receive in educational or medical work within the service of Christian bodies, and that of the minister or evangelist. The disparity is far greater than in the West. Standards are set by education or medicine generally, there are government grants—the reasons are obvious but the difficulty remains. Now, if a mission follows, let us say, the Nevius [4] method (insisting on immediate self-support of each congregation and spending money only on the missionary and his personal secretary) there is the danger that the actual ordained leadership of the church may comprise almost no one of the caliber of the educational and medical workers. Accordingly there are many (of whom I am one) who feel that it is possible to press a theory

[4] See the *International Review of Missions*, April 1935, " The Nevius Methods," by Dr. C. A. Clark.

so far as to do harm, and that it is not an improper use of missionary funds to make possible the appointment on modest but reasonable salary of a certain number of men of outstanding quality, provided that they are not regarded as mission appointed men and thus of a higher grade—for such regard can only depreciate the church's own estimation of itself—and that the whole matter is carried out within the total church scheme.

There remain two matters on which something should be said : the unity of the church and the challenge to the principle of evangelism represented by the accusation of proselytism, and the more or less syncretistic theories which usually accompany it.

Of the unity of the church what can I say but that we are most of us still shamefully complaisant in the face of a denial of what we profess ? Let it be admitted—not grudgingly, but with full conviction—that the historic breaches in the unity of the church of Christ have had their meaning and their necessity. I at least am not among those who apologize for the Reformation, and though I would not cross the road to convert a man to Presbyterianism I shall continue a Presbyterian until I know that the values for which it stands are conserved in a wider unity. And let it be admitted further that it is not only the Western Christians but the Christians of the younger churches (and some of the ancient ones like the Syrians of Malabar) who know how to invent and to love division.

Can it be denied, when all this has been said, that the major part of the responsibility for the divided state of the church in the East lies with us who have not only taken our divisions there—for that perhaps could not have been avoided—but have been culpably slow in recognizing that the persistence of divisions whose historical meaning is, at least in many cases, irrelevant to the Eastern lands is a menace to the life of the church? Not many missionaries would deny this, and they have done their share manfully in the labor for reunion. But there are pillars of the church in the Western lands who see so clearly the value of what they and their fathers have stood for that they can see little else, and who are not ashamed to bring pressure on the younger churches in favor of their own loyalties. It is perhaps only a minor point that there can be no truly *indigenous* church so long as the foreign names with their alien history persist, though some part of the reason for the large number of Christians in the East, notably in China, who pay no regard to the church at all, must be found here. The deep tragedy lies in the fact that in a day of the Lord when, in the face of all the powers of earth and hell, the gospel witness is to be proclaimed, we offer a divided fellowship. I shall not forget the day when I sat with a group of Christians, drawn from the four principal churches (excluding that of Rome) in Travancore, discussing and praying over the great turning to Christ among the Ezhavas. One aged Syrian priest said to me that if his church, with all its thousand and more years of history, should fail through conservative prejudice to welcome these newcomers, the judgment of God ought to fall upon it. But—one could never forget that to those who in the community of a Hindu loyalty were united we were offering four churches.

Close cooperation and all such work as that of the National Christian councils can do much to mitigate the evils of division, but, as one who spends his days in promoting such cooperation, I would say without a shadow of hesitation that it is not a substitute for the united church of Christ.

If they ask us, " Is Christ divided ? " must we say, " Well, yes and no " ?

The other matter is not less fundamental. It is put most clearly by Mr. Gandhi, who holds that as in clothes and food and customs, so in religion, a man should hold by the stuff of his own people—*swadeshi*. He deeply resents, in spite of his personal friendliness to Christian missionaries, the fact that they will not be content to teach and heal but will also " proselytize." The value of the work, in his judgment, is destroyed ; it is not disinterested, as the Bhagavad Gita tells us our actions should be. That is one aspect of the problem, the practical one. On the other hand, we have the type of religious thinking, ultimately rooted in a monistic view of reality, for which the future holds a synthesis of the world's faiths, and which therefore looks on " conversion " and " evangelism " as belonging to a conservative and slightly illiterate world. These ideas have an appeal, apart from their intrinsic worth, to some of the most sensitive spirits in the missionary movement, who hate the very thought of aggressiveness and superiority.

But the answer is surely very clear and simple. No Christian offers teaching or medical help as a bait so that the evangelistic hook may be swallowed. It is an expression of the love and compassion of Christ, and it is a part of that lifting up of the Son of

Man which is to be until the end of time. But neither does he offer the Christian gospel as something which connotes his own superiority. He does not say, " Copy my superior culture." He says, " Believe on the Lord Jesus Christ who gave himself for you." We cannot better St. Paul, in his missionary charter, " We preach not ourselves but Christ Jesus our Lord, and ourselves your servants for Jesus' sake."

I do not for a moment deny that we should do well to study the charges made against the missionary movement—that it cares too much for numbers and that it uses unfair methods, that it is apathetic to national culture, or that its massive organization suggests the waging of a military campaign. But I contend that there is in the very heart of the Christian gospel that which will always give rise to the witness of evangelism, for if you believe with all your heart and mind that the Son of God loved you and gave himself for you and for all mankind with an undistinguishing regard, who are you that you should be silent on such a matter?

VIII

THE CHURCH AND THE SOCIAL ORDER

THROUGHOUT the whole of the East the question presses home upon the Christian church and is echoed most earnestly by the younger generation : " What is the Christian message for the social order ? In the face of the social need around us, what ought the church, what ought Christians, to do ? "

We turn now to what is not the least perplexing of the problems discussed in this book. The difficulties to be faced are of three kinds. In the first place, there is going on all over the Eastern countries (as in Africa) a profound social change which affects every part of life. In the second place, the Christian church is very small in relation to the immensity of the tasks that have to be faced. In the third place, much of the needed action must be taken, and can only be taken, by governments, and is entirely beyond the reach of private bodies, even if they were far more powerful than the church can claim to be anywhere in the East.

Perhaps it may be well to begin by dispelling a still common illusion, namely, that the linking of the life of the East with that of the West through the extension of a common economic order is altogether bad. It is often spoken of solely in terms of exploitation or materialism ; a simple and on the whole satisfactory order of society is being ousted, so it is suggested, by another whose main motive power is the greed of the wealthier nations ; the simplicity and spiritual quality of village life is contrasted with the horrors of mine and factory in lands hardly yet provided with those poor checks which the social conscience has imposed upon industrialism in the West.

Of course there is truth in this reproach, but there is much that is purely sentimental delusion. A machine-using civilization may be a spiritual one ; a primitive civilization may be, for the mass of mankind, scarcely above the animal level. The first thing that strikes the most casual visitor to the East is the spectacle of men, and women too, performing tasks which beasts perform in other lands. Where great populations press upon the land and hunger is never far away a burden rests upon human shoulders which people in Western lands hardly understand. Perhaps a slightly sensitive tourist may feel a twinge of understanding when he steps into a rickshaw and is pulled away to his destination by a human horse. The beautiful handicrafts of China are justly praised, but still more wonderful is the contrast between the artistic capacity of the workman and his tolerance of the most indescribable working conditions. Writing of primitive industry and transport in China, Mr. J. B. Tayler says :

In all this industry there is nothing to spare the muscles. One watches the beating out of ingots of iron, or pairs of laborers bathed in perspiration spending days sawing planks out of big logs that a band saw would reduce in an hour or two ; elsewhere it may be coolies fighting for the privilege of carrying heavy loads a day's journey for the cost of a few bowls of rice. In the north, much of the traffic is by wheelbarrow. Waiting at a wayside inn at dusk on a dry frosty winter's evening one is deafened by the strident creaking of the large wooden wheels as the barrowmen arrive. Singly and in groups they continue to drop in well on into the night. Their barrows, with loads up to four hundredweights, are left in the unflagged courtyard. . . . Before dawn the next morning they are on the road again, not breakfasting until perhaps ten or eleven o'clock, passing the day on two meals only. In this way they tramp hour after hour with but brief rests, pushing and balancing their heavy loads in the grooves worn by others before them, crossing and recrossing the cart roads, with their deep ruts smothered in inches of dust, mounting banks several feet high by the roadside or crossing a plowed field to cut off a corner ; with nothing to save their muscles except when they can mount a sail. So they go on, it may be through biting wind, in twenty or thirty degrees of frost or in blinding dust that penetrates and envelops everything, day in, day out, until they have covered the hundred miles or more from Shantung to some city of the north.[1]

Such a system—and something like this has been the lot of the masses of Asia for centuries—supplies little more than an animal existence and keeps those engaged in it from rising much above the level of the beast of burden.

Or one thinks of the millions of lives lost in famines, and of all that transport means at such times, when grain can be rapidly shifted from one area to

[1] J. B. Tayler, *Farm and Factory in China*, p. 40.

another by modern railways ; or of modern medicine, which is a part of modern civilization. The Western physician, be he missionary or government officer or private practitioner, who comes into contact with the measureless physical need of the Eastern masses, is not likely to be under any illusions about the amenities of life possible to those masses under the conditions of the older and more primitive society.

But it is just as untrue to assume that to take the machine age to the East is to confer upon the East an unquestioned blessing. Possibly this error is less prevalent in our self-conscious and self-critical society than it used to be. It is not so long since one used to link the blessings of Western civilization with the Christian gospel in an unquestioned unity. The two things went together. Of course it was better for the Eastern peoples to have " civilization " ; of course it must be for their good that the social institutions of the West should be planted among them. The reflective minds among us are not now so sure about these things. But whatever the reflective minds may think, the great process goes on. It moves with a kind of impersonal force and momentum. The quest for markets, the lure of cheap labor, the need of raw material and the growth of capitalist and entrepreneur groups in the Eastern countries themselves, all make it inevitable that the mass populations of the East and of Africa should be drawn within the world economy, which is virtually a Western economy. As we have seen, there is good in this, and it can hardly be wrong to see in so great a movement, rooted as it is in the essential capacities of mankind to understand and master the secrets of nature, something in which God is at work. But just because the great movement must go on, it is as important to see clearly the bad in it as to see the good.

First, there are the grosser evils. We have described the drudgery and suffering of the old order ; what are we to say of the factories and mines of the new ? Here is an extract from the report of the Child Labor Commission of Shanghai [2] (1924), giving an account of the conditions of work prevailing in the silk filatures, where the great majority of the employees were women and children and only a few were boys :

> The children brush the cocoons and prepare them for the reelers by removing the waste and so exposing the silk thread. This operation is performed over basins containing nearly boiling water, with which the fingers of the children frequently and necessarily come into contact, thereby becoming roughened and unsightly. Many of the children are very young, being not more than six years of age. In the Shanghai district the children almost invariably stand at work, five or six hours at a stretch. Owing to the presence of the hot water in the basins the temperature of the workroom is always considerably above the normal and the atmosphere is very humid. It was stated that fainting in hot weather is not uncommon. The children earn from twenty to twenty-five silver cents a day. In the main they present a pitiable sight. Their physical condition is poor, and their faces are devoid of any expression of happiness or well-being.

[2] In the work done in connection with this commission the National Christian Council and the Y.W.C.A. of China played a highly important part.

They appear to be miserable, both physically and mentally. . . . The Commission is satisfied that the conditions under which these children are employed are indefensible.[3]

If this picture is thought to be out of date (though little has been done by legislation combined with effective inspection to alter it) here is Professor Tawney's more recent account :

> With the exception of certain individual establishments . . . the conditions generally obtaining in factory employment recall those of the first, and worst, phase of the Industrial Revolution in England. Not only are hours preposterously long, and wages almost incredibly low, but part of the work is often done by relays of cheap or unpaid juvenile workers, sometimes imported from the country, and occasionally, it is alleged, actually sold to their employers, in shops which are frequently little better than barns, and in which the most elementary conditions of health and safety appear to be ignored. It is possible, in certain cities, to go through a succession of these little establishments, which may or may not be technically factories, largely staffed with boys between eight and sixteen years of age, working twelve to fourteen hours per day for seven days in the week, and sleeping at night on the floor of the shop, in which the lighting is such as to make it certain that the sight of many of them will be permanently injured, machinery is completely unguarded, the air is loaded with poisonous dust, which there is no ventilation to remove, and the buildings are unprovided, in spite of municipal by-laws, with emergency exits, with

[3] *Humanity and Labor in China*, pp. 153–54. The whole report can be seen in Cmd. 2442.

the result that, in the event of fire, some proportion of the workers will almost certainly be burned.[4]

Here is a testimony from India, describing the *chawls* in tenement houses in which the Bombay millworker lives :

Land is exceedingly valuable and the people live in gloomy tenements, often four or five stories high, with primitive sanitation, rambling passages and stairways from floor to floor that are little better than ladders. Up under the roof on the top-most story, an adult may not be able to stand upright and many rooms have little or no natural light. . . . One-roomed dwellings are the rule in most Indian working class quarters, but it was surprising even in Bombay to find four families living in the four corners of a room, while a fifth found accommodation on a high table which turned one corner into a two-story dwelling.[5]

Anyone who studies these questions soon finds pathetic illustrations of the truth that we are members one of another, for the increasing unity of the economic order produces some strange results. For instance, the acuteness of the slump in America cut the Japanese silk export to pieces, and one effect was that in the terrible distress that followed numbers of Japanese girls sold themselves into prostitution to support their families.

But apart from these obvious and terrible evils there is the not less important fact of the deep and subtle change that is being wrought in the life and culture of the people, not merely in the towns but in

[4] *Land and Labor in China*, pp. 149–50.
[5] M. Cécile Matheson, *Indian Industry*, p. 40.

the villages. It is a familiar story now that the rail-
way, the motor bus, the wireless, the cheap newspaper
and the like have gone far to break down the aloofness of the Asiatic village. They have broken down
much else. The old family organization of life in
China and the caste order of India are both weakened by the implicit individualism that comes with
the newer conditions. An experienced missionary
in China pointed out to me the rise in the practice
of life insurance in China as an example of the growing individualism. An Indian Christian wrote to me
from the north India city in which he was engaged
as a social worker :

> To earn their livelihood villagers have left the
> villages for the big cities and for other provinces—
> Bombay, Calcutta, Cawnpore, Assam, Malay,
> Burma—going there without wives and often set-
> tling down in the new places where there are no
> longer the restraints of the *panchayat* (village
> court) and moral sanctions of society. Caste is
> losing its old force ; marriages are made in other
> castes, as advertised in the newspapers. In these
> days Brahmans are working in leather trades and
> as carpenters, blacksmiths and weavers, trades once
> considered taboo. Railway traveling rubs the cor-
> ners off, people eat in restaurants with their shoes
> on and without a ceremonial bath before eating.
> The joint family system, owing to these things, is
> being disintegrated ; the village entity is disappear-
> ing because the people are moving to the towns
> and establishing relationships with city people.

This kind of thing could be quoted from every part
of the East. The effects are not all bad ; new ideas
of sanitation make their way ; if the old religion is

weakened (as everywhere it is) there is less of the superstition which obstructed health and cleanliness. Most of all, the new social world is one in which the evils of society are known, discussed and reprobated, and in which their extinction is planned. Not only the evils of the factory area but the sufferings of the peasant are now understood by earnest men and women who want to " do something about it."

Hence, I think, the rise of communism in the East. In neither China nor India is it solely, or even primarily, an urban affair. It has its roots in the condition of the rural masses, illuminated by the socially quickened consciousness of educated people from the towns. I have already quoted Professor Tawney's verdict on Chinese communism.[6] Pandit Jawaharlal Nehru's autobiography affords from the Indian side a graphic account of the rise of communistic ideas in the desperate villages of the United Provinces. It is in industrialized Japan, where industry as contrasted with agriculture embraces almost half of the population, that communism has had an urban setting.

It is plain that some of the greatest problems that confront the student of changing society in the East can be solved only by state action. That does not mean that states may not be induced to act by the force of opinion, but it does mean that for some of the evils that afflict the masses the efforts of private reformers can do little. Consider, for example, the problems of tenancy and of agricultural debt. One of the features of rural life in all Asia is the struggle of the farmer to keep or to get hold of the land. China

[6] See Chap. II.

has had a stronger tradition of the owner-farmer than either India or Japan, but even there Professor J. L. Buck estimates that not more than from a half to three-fifths of the cultivators are owners and from a fifth to a quarter part owner and part tenant. There are figures for the whole country, but while in the drought and famine stricken Yellow river region in the north the owner percentage is as high as 69, in the wealthier region of the Yangtse valley and the south it is only 32, and in the rich provinces of Chekiang, Kwangtung and Fukien, occupied with overseas trade, it is respectively 27, 30 and 9. Plainly, in regions where the accumulation of wealth is possible, there has been a buying up of farms.

In Japan it is stated that 31 per cent of the farmers are owners, 27 per cent tenants and 42 per cent part owner and part tenant. There have been thousands of tenant strikes and refusals to pay the rent.

In India there is a variety of systems of land tenure, but it is roughly true that in the north there is the big landlord or *zamindari* system and in the south the small-holder or *ryotwari* system. In India—the same is true to some extent in Japan and China—there is the additional evil of the excessive fragmentation of holdings through the operation of laws of inheritance. The economic working of the land of India demands some comprehensive measure of consolidation of holdings to make profitable farming possible.

Agricultural debt is a staggering fact in India. In the Panjab, for example, the total cultivated land amounts to about thirty million acres. The annual land revenue chargeable on this area is about fifty million rupees. The *interest* on the debt owed on account of the land is nearly two hundred million rupees annually. It is difficult to see how this debt can be paid and how there can be any rural prosperity under these conditions. In Japan it is officially stated that the average debt of a farming family is about £55, but some economists hold that the true figures are higher and that the total farm debt is now between £500 and £600 millions, whereas twenty years ago it was £40 millions.

These are only examples—no more is possible within the scope of this book—to show the nature of the rural problems in these Eastern lands. One need not be surprised to find that radical ideas on the handling of rural economics meet with a ready welcome. The problem clearly must be faced ; if not, nothing can stay the growth of desperate discontent.

There is, however, much that can be done even within the present system to pave the way for better things. Both in India and in China, and to a smaller degree in Japan, vigorous efforts have been made during the last few years to bring a fresh coherence into Christian work in the rural areas. The attention given to this subject at the Jerusalem meeting of the International Missionary Council in 1928, with the work of Dr. Kenyon Butterfield throughout the East immediately after it, did a great deal to clear the corporate mind of the churches and missions on the question of right policy and method. With some differences in detail the main line of development in India and in China has been much the same. It is what in India is called the " rural reconstruction unit." Put less formally, it is a plan to unite the home, the church, the school, the hospital and the credit bank—five basal institutions of the corporate life—in a plan for the creation of a better rural society. I include the church as central to any Christian village plan, but the same central ideas are operative in government circles and indeed among all who work for the uplift of the villages. Indeed there is no department of work in which in India and China alike there is so ample opportunity for close collaboration on the part of Christian bodies, governments and private agencies.

In India it means the restoration of the broken unity of village life, through the revival of the old village courts and the recovery of village industries, with which Mr. Gandhi and his campaign for homespun cloth have been so greatly concerned. Education for the village is the subject of endless discussion, and in devising right ways of training village teachers and relating curricula to the experience and needs of village children missionary training schools have an honorable record. Adult education and the reduction of adult mass illiteracy are in the front of the picture in India as in China. The rural credit bank and cooperative society have long played an important part in India in reducing the burden of debt, though many missions know to their cost how much easier it is to lend money when the society starts than to recover it as time demands repayment. The provision of a better health service is vital, and there are increasing numbers of medical missionaries and Indian Christian physicians who wish to develop the Christian ministry of healing especially in the villages through simple methods of itinerant medical work.

The central idea of the unit plan is to take a group

of villages, reasonably contiguous, and through the five organs—home, church, school, bank and hospital or dispensary—to work coherently toward a stronger community. It is plain that such cooperative planning is vital to the growth of the rural Christian churches, apart from its bearing on general state plans for rural advancement. If the already large communities of rural Christians drawn from the bottom social groups should greatly increase, as I have shown to be likely, this complete rural method will become even more important, for on it will depend the possibility of self-supporting churches.

In China, notably in the province of Kiangsi from which the communist forces had been driven, the government has undertaken a great piece of rural reconstruction, and has been notably aided by the church in the rural experimental center at Lichwan. Village cooperative societies have been started on a considerable scale by the China International Famine Relief Commission, with full backing from the government. These societies have been valuable also in teaching the people to work together in various types of reconstructive work, such as better communications, better village schools and the promotion of health measures. At Nanking there is under the charge of Dr. J. Lossing Buck what is perhaps the finest center of rural study and research under Christian auspices in any part of Asia.

In Japan, as we have seen, the church has been urban to a far greater extent than in India or China. Of the twelve hundred missionaries in Japan not more than a hundred are in rural areas. But now far more attention is devoted to rural needs, and the methods of the Danish folk high schools, so influential as an example to the whole world, are being assiduously studied by Japanese Christians. They have noted that in Denmark there is no sense of inferiority among the Danish farmers, who are proud of their rural life, and those who work among the Japanese villages are urged to acquire " the rural mind."

At this point we may note a development in China which may become an example to other parts of the East. It is generally agreed that the prosperity of China demands an increase in industrial production, and it has been too easily assumed that this means necessarily the big factory with its concentration of labor. Professor Tayler has been the leader in a most interesting movement, the object of which has been to assist village industries, or industries which though not strictly " village " can be carried on with the minimum disturbance of home and village life, by bringing to them such technical help as may enable them to hold their own even against the competition of the mass factory. He has helped to develop woolen industries and pottery making in North China in such a way as to preserve village life while greatly increasing the economic resources of the peasant. It would seem to a layman that along this line there must be a future. The hunger of the masses of Asia (India has seen her population increase by over one hundred millions since the beginning of the nineteenth century) [7] cannot be assuaged without an increase in industry, but it must be possible to de-

---

[7] The population of the world has increased in that period by over one thousand millions, but this has been chiefly in the industrialized countries.

velop industry without the appalling effects upon national and individual life that follow upon the great festering aggregations of population in the factory and mill centers. Here is one of the spheres where the application of a measure of technical skill to the problems may work wonders.

In the great mining and factory areas it is not easy to point to outstanding efforts on the part of Christian bodies. There are notable pieces of work, such as settlements and " neighborhood houses " in Bombay and Cawnpore, in Osaka and Shanghai, and many brave men and women have devoted themselves with absolute self-forgetfulness to improving the conditions of these places. Much of the welfare work carried on by the great firms is put into the hands of missions or of the Young Men's and Young Women's Christian associations, and the Y.W.C.A. in particular has a rather notable record of pioneer work in this field. But even when all this is said, it is still true that in proportion to the size and gravity of the problem too little is done.

Undoubtedly it is to legislation that we must look for some of the most important action. The Washington convention of 1919 resulted in a series of proposals for the regulation of the hours and labor of women and children (to take the most important items) which were carried into law in India and later in Japan, and the Chinese factory laws go in theory even further. But laws are useless without sanction for enforcement, and the conditions in China (in which extra-territoriality must be included) have made it difficult for the Chinese government to invest its industrial codes with the stern aspect of reality.

Even the Japanese laws are accompanied by an ominous number of exceptive clauses, and in India, where on the whole labor protective legislation is in advance of anything in the East, all depends on the number of inspectors and that again upon provincial finance.

Trade unions—the principal method, when all is said, by which the Western working class has sought to protect itself—have come into being in the East, but not yet in any strength.   In Japan they live a somewhat dangerous life under the present regime ; in China, says Professor Tawney, the trade union act, " while recognizing the right of association, surrounds it with restrictions which appear to deprive it of much of its value." [8]   In India trade unions are stronger, but the movement is split between a communist section and a moderate group, and is in many parts still the plaything of politicians.

Here, then, is one of the major unsolved questions of our time.   It is fundamentally the same as that which vexes the mind of thoughtful Christians in every country of the Western world.   What is the Christian message and the duty of the church in the face of these social facts ?

I dislike the antithesis " Christianity or communism," for it suggests that Christianity belongs to the same genus as communism but is a better variety. Yet there is truth in the slogan, for communism claims to explain the economic phenomena of the modern world and to offer a certain hope of their alteration based upon a view of reality, and Christianity likewise is an all-embracing faith based upon a

[8] *Land and Labor in China*, p. 151.

doctrine of reality. There ought, it is felt, to be a definite Christian social doctrine and social program.

Toyohiko Kagawa, if I understand him aright, would say that there is such a definite Christian social doctrine and program in the cooperative movement. In his hands it has gone far beyond the consumers' cooperative societies which are most familiar to the Western world, and beyond the rural credit and marketing organizations of India and China. In a letter referring primarily to his new medical cooperative society Kagawa says:

> The whole movement for the establishment of Christian society through the cooperatives is what I call the modern brotherhood movement. Medical cooperatives are one small subitem in it, included in the much wider general heading of mutual aid cooperatives. Besides these there are insurance cooperatives, credit unions, producers' cooperatives, marketing cooperatives and utility cooperatives, as well as the kind most familiar to you in Britain, consumers' cooperatives. Only when all these seven varieties of cooperatives shall have been thoroughly established and are interlocking, in international as well as national worldwide absorption of activities now carried on by private competition and in the old laissez faire manner, *shall we as Christians have an adequate message for the communists.*[9]

Dr. Kagawa has a philosophy of cooperative economics which I will try to summarize in words taken from his own writings. Matter, he says, has no mean-

[9] Italics mine.

ing as a commodity unless it touches the following seven points : purpose or aim ; order or law ; selection or efficiency ; growth ; exchange ; energy or power ; life at its highest. The seven types of cooperative mentioned above yield the seven psychological values required. Consumers' cooperatives touch life at the point of *purpose* or aim in getting food and other material necessities for an advancing civilization ; producers' cooperatives deal with and release *energy* and power for production ; credit cooperatives provide for *growth,* as capital is necessary for economic enterprise ; marketing cooperatives secure an adequate system of *exchange ;* mutual aid, utility and insurance cooperatives provide for *efficiency* in the selection of the higher values in life which the whole movement tries to create for the benefit of all. All cooperatives promote *law and order* by smoothing out local, national and international difficulties in the economic and social realm.[10]

I have stated Dr. Kagawa's view at length because he is the only Christian in the East who has offered a Christian doctrine and method on a question of burning importance, and because he himself and his followers believe that he has found something of world importance. I am not qualified, nor is it possible within the limits of this little book, to criticize Kagawa's views in detail, but it is only honest to indicate something of the line along which one believes the forward path lies.

The communists are right as against a great deal of current Christianity. It is perfectly true (and an

[10] See, e.g., *Japan Christian Quarterly,* spring, 1935.

important part of the case against communism) that in the communist view there is no place for individual freedom. But if, as our Lord would have us do, we judge by actions and not by words, we cannot deny that the present economic order does not conspicuously care about individual worth and freedom, and that a great many Christians have in fact assented to this *practice* while insisting in *words* upon the infinite worth of the individual. Religion which does not seek to express its deepest insights by appropriate effort in the stern field of action can hardly hope to escape the charge (to use the language of Professor Macmurray) that it is only pseudo-religion.

But the most common version of Christian social thinking, at least in the Anglo-Saxon world, the school of liberal social Christianity, is open to a different but not less fatal criticism. It has not taken sin seriously. It has been based upon an optimistic view of human nature. " It has insisted that good will can establish justice, whatever the political and economic mechanisms may be. It has insisted on this futile moralism at a moment in history when the whole world faces disaster because the present methods of production and distribution are no longer able to maintain the peace and order of society." [11] I find it hard not to believe that Kagawa, for instance, claims too much for his cooperatives if they are thought of not only as ways whereby Christians may together express their corporate life but as a substitute for the controlling power of a right social mechanism.

If, then, a Christianity that is merely withdrawn from radical concern with the social problem is

[11] Reinhold Niebuhr, *An Interpretation of Christian Ethics*, p. 181.

wrong, and if we are not less at fault if we regard Christian moral effort and persuasion as enough, are we limited to the view that nothing matters but action in the political realm ?

I think not. This rough sketch, covering so slightly a vast territory, has at least shown that. What have we seen ? Efforts, especially in the rural field, to express common Christian life in a better social order— weak and imperfect, it may be, but each one a little oasis in the desert of hunger, debt, disease and illiteracy, making the good news of Christ *real* in the face of earthly need. Efforts again, whether by individuals or groups or societies, to denounce and expose evil, so that those who are in charge of the engine of government may be stirred, or to suggest the lines along which governmental action might be taken.[12] Behind all this, the continuous life of a community, the church, at its worst no more than a self-regarding society, but at its best the source of dynamic life and hope and changed men and women.

It is in a combination of these three things that hope for the future lies. To go back to the principles stated again and again in this book, realistic Christianity demands the recognition of a tension between the absolute demand of God upon the human soul, the law of love, universal and perfect, and the best society that can be devised in our sinful world. To believe that by our effort and devotion we can, as so often we loosely say, " establish the kingdom of heaven on earth " is to forget that it is God who

[12] Perhaps the most notable instance is the work of the International Missionary Council's commission of inquiry into the conditions in the Rhodesian copper belt. See *Modern Industry and the African,* by J. Merle Davis.

establishes his kingdom, and to fall into the profound error of communism, that a human society can be produced which is beyond the need of redemption. Along that path, no matter how devoted and selfless the effort put forth, nothing lies but a secularized church, lost in the multitude of its own service to man. But we must nevertheless continuously strive to put into action every insight we get from God. Every little Christian community, every bit of Christian service to the poor and oppressed, if it is rooted in humble reliance upon God, is a testimony within the earthly order to that diviner order by which earthly things are always to be judged. The economic sphere of life is to be the continual scene of efforts by Christians to make real their religious insight and conviction. A religion that within a world of sin and need testifies to the absolute law of love only by words is condemned. Knowing always that within this world the absolute law of love will ever be beyond them, Christians will strive none the less to carry it into the heart of their practice. It is a paradox, but only to those who view it from without.

Secondly, they will take their part in the work of secular government. To say that no governmental system can be perfect is not to say that all are equally good or bad. That is the better system which goes furthest to make possible the realization by men of the Christian values and standards of life. Christians are acutely divided on this question ; ideal fascism, ideal communism and ideal democracy—each is offered to us as the type of state most congruous with the Christian insights. The struggle among these systems is one in which Christians are vitally con-

cerned. Leaving aside the political aspects,[13] it is an
important part of the Christian witness to protest
against social evil, to denounce oppression, and to
seek by every means of public education and persuasion to make the legal and political structure of a
country such as is just. A valuable work can be done
by accurate and informed exposure of facts.

But it is in the last resort with the life of the church
itself that the Christian social witness is mainly bound
up. It is for it to serve the world by producing men
and women who have the spirit and the insight that
it needs. Thus it will fill with power the social activities and experiments it may conduct. Thus it will
add to what state action can do the subtle ways of
personal service. Most of all, being a community of
people bound together as persons in common love
and service to God and to one another, it will witness
by its life to the kingdom of which it is in some
sense the earnest and token.

Professor Wieman, of Chicago, sums up the matter :

The early church was not primarily an instrumental association. It was not first of all devoted
to service or good works. We do not find that it
concentrated its efforts immediately on providing
wholesome recreation, or fighting political corrup-
tion, or bringing justice into the economic system,

[13] I would say on this point only that a democratic system seems
to me plainly best by Christian standards, provided political freedom
is accompanied by economic. The other two systems appear to be
attempts to reintegrate a disintegrating society by recourse to an
absolute authority. The democratic statesman must therefore not
merely repel communism and fascism but address himself to the
problem which the fascist and communist try to solve.

or improving the schools, or opposing slavery, or doing any good works in marked degree except to dispense charity. It was organic rather than instrumental. It was an association devoted to saving souls ; that is, it fostered, enriched and exalted the individualities of its members until these outcasts, these downtrodden and crushed, these slaves and riffraff rose up in towering strength to dominate the age. Such magnified and developed personalities could and did, in the course of time, enter into instrumental association for the purpose of doing good works, removing causes of evil, transforming conditions and reconstructing the world. We do not mean to suggest that the church should refrain from good works. On the contrary, it should do even more than it is doing. It should be an instrumental association as well as organic. But first of all, we claim, it should be organic. Its first and greatest function in the world is to bring people together in such a way that they can interact in deep organic community, with profound mutual understanding. It should quicken to life and to abundant growth those impulses, aspirations and personal attitudes wherein the individual comes to largest fulfillment of his utmost possibilities. This is individual salvation ; but it is also profoundly social.[14]

[14] H. N. Wieman, *Methods of Private Religious Living*, pp. 145–46.

IX

CONCLUSION

ALMOST every day one meets somebody who has just read the foreign page of the London *Times* and feels that " the world is in a terrible mess." A good many people get no further than this, and it is a commonplace that the saturation of the public mind with news of suffering and horror during ~ ~~ ever since the World War has brought with it a certain callousness. I have never forgotten the sorrowful remark of the secretary of one of the greatest missionary societies who, after outlining a case of need and opportunity which was likely to go by default because money could not be found, said, " The trouble is not that people don't know but that they don't really care."

Nothing could be further from the Christian mind than this. The Christian view is still the prophetic view. Jeremiah and his fellows were not content to say that things were in a mess—as in their time they undoubtedly were. The prophetic voice sought to find in the events of the world the mind and will of God, and to call men to repent and obey, no matter how terrible the cost of the obedience.

We need this attitude today. The purpose of this book is to show, no matter how imperfectly nor with what ignorance and dogmatism, that we live in a day of the Lord. Quite unashamedly I have taken the church as the key to the situation, for I believe that the witness of the divine community in the world takes us nearer than anything else to the meaning of history. Who cares about the Assyrians and their conquests now, or for the glories of Babylon? What mattered then was the fate of an obscure pair of Syrian kingdoms. The groups of outcasts and " base things of the world " that began the witness of the church in Europe outlasted the Roman Empire, to which they must have seemed utterly insignificant. Who can say that the witness of Christians today in Japan or in Manchuria, in China, in the Indian villages, in Iran or Turkey or Egypt, may not in the judgment of history seem far greater in importance than any of the events which today fill men's eyes? It is idle to dream, but it is not idle to choose the standard by which you will live and judge and be judged.

In a world of change, full of menace, with new gods arising as the twilight embraces the old, these scattered Christian communities live out their lives. Some of them face the prospect of annihilation. Some face possibilities of immense growth. Some are almost asleep. But all are parts of the universal church, and the varied situations of which an account has been given in this book do not relate only to them but to the whole church throughout the world. What of the Western churches in this day? Is there in these Eastern conflicts a word of God not only to the churches of those lands but to those of the West also?

Let us look first at the secular problems that confront us. I have written critically of the Japanese policy, and it is therefore all the more necessary to say that the Western powers, not least Great Britain,

are not guiltless of forcing Japan into a mood of bitterness and self-assertiveness in defense against an
" encirclement " such as Germany believed herself
caught in before the World War. As far back as the
framing of the Covenant of the League of Nations,
the Japanese sought to secure the incorporation of a
clause which would definitely assert racial equality.[1]
The request was rejected at the instance of the British
empire, and when brought up a second time as a part
of the preamble to the Covenant it was again rejected,
with the British empire leading the opposition. (The
fact that it was Australian pressure that led to this
result does not exonerate the representatives of Great
Britain.) So judicious an observer as Professor Toynbee [2] is of the opinion that the anti-Japanese trade
regulations, while defensible up to a point in view
of unemployment in Lancashire and the dislocated
state of world trade, did definitely increase in Japan
the sense of being alone in the world with all men's
hands against her.

This is but one instance, and there are countless
others in the history of the relationships between the
Western powers and those of the East. Or take the
issue of race relationships. I have said almost nothing
of the subject in this book, but it is of the highest
importance. I am thinking not only of the iniquities
of color-bar legislation and the like, but of the existence of racial pride and antipathy within the church
itself. Islam is not slow to make the most of this
weakness. Years ago the Moslems in South Africa
began to invite Africans to embrace Islam on the

[1] The facts are given in Zimmern, *The League of Nations and the
Rule of Law*, Part II, Chap. X.

[2] See *Survey of International Affairs*, 1934, p. 666.

ground, among other claims, that it offered racial equality, unlike Christianity which perpetuated the white man's dominance. In Travancore, where there is the great movement among the Ezhavas toward Christianity, a recent convert from Hinduism to Islam declared, at a great meeting of Ezhavas, that in Islam alone was there real brotherhood without distinction of color or race or caste.

But what of the relation between these younger churches in the East and the older churches of the West ? What is demanded of Western Christians ?

First, there is need of genuine knowledge. It is really amazing to find how little interest is taken in the dramatic facts of modern church history by Christian people, not excluding a large number of clergy and ministers. Even when there is interest there is often little knowledge ; sentiment and the desire to hear of great successes and startling facts obscure the realities. How many missionaries on coming home have longed to tell the real facts—the difficulties and disappointments, the perplexities and anxieties—but have felt that the facts were not wanted.

It should never be forgotten that the Christian church, in all its parts taken together throughout the whole of the East, is a very small thing. Its weaknesses and the limitations under which it labors have, I hope, been fairly stated in these pages. A critical judge would perhaps accuse me of overstating what can be expected from the churches as they are now. There is an abundance of criticism of them among the keener young in the East, as there is of the churches in the West. To some Chinese Christians it would seem that much of what is written at the close of the last chapter is pure wishful thinking. I have seen enough of the magnificent quality of the best native leaders of Eastern Christianity to be sure that my emphases are not wrong. But, I repeat, the churches we are talking about, beset by the same great struggle between communism and fascism as the churches of the West, wrestling with far greater problems of witness and interpretation than the churches of the West, are, compared with them, very weak and small. It is one of the dramatic facts of this day in which we live that this tiny, weak, scattered and divided church is the spearhead of strife and the center of controversy in so much of the world. We need to know, far more of us, the facts about it.

Second, help in the form of personal service is needed. Most of the great missionary societies have today many vacancies, for which no candidates can be found though funds to send them are available. The forms under which the work of the missionary is now carried on differ greatly from those of fifty or a hundred years ago, but the missionary is still wanted. I can find no faltering of accent in the voices that send this call to us from the East. That they know what sort of people they want, that they ask for helpers and not masters, we have all heard. But I know of no responsible Christian leaders in Japan, China, India or the Near East who would dream of denying that for the tasks to which the church is called in these lands the indigenous local bodies are far too weak, and that as they are tasks for the church universal they must have the help of the wider Christendom.

More and more, therefore (I say nothing here

that is not a truism to every missionary society) the
mission becomes quite frankly the link between the
church in the East and the church in the West.   An
Anglican priest who goes out under the Society for
the Propagation of the Gospel or the Church Missionary Society to China will find himself more conscious of his place as a priest in the Chung Hwa Sheng
Kung Hwei than of his status as a missionary.   That
would not be the case in all countries, but it is with
that sort of status that we shall be concerned more
and more in the future.   There is a conscious longing among all who bear the burden of leadership in
the indigenous churches for personal Christian service, rendered in the spirit of love and brotherhood,
backed by as good professional qualifications as a man
or woman can acquire, and inspired by the love of
Christ.

   But this is only a part of the personal service that
is desired and possible.   The missionaries are only a
fraction of the great number of men and women who
go to the East in the services, on business, in the pro-
fessions, and along all the well trodden avenues where
the peoples of the nations walk and meet one another.
Even today, when it is becoming common form in
the East to make a sharp distinction between Christianity and Western civilization, these people are
regarded as Christians.   Some of them are, and there
is hardly any witness that compares with that of the
Christian layman in business or official life who is not
afraid to make his ordinary life the vehicle of his
testimony.   More of them, perhaps, have been Christians and have lost the way.   The curious artificiality
of European life in the East, and the temptations

incidental to it, play havoc with many who, it may be, have not been well enough grounded to stand by themselves in an atmosphere where conventions are opposed to outspoken Christian profession. The care of the oversea European is a vital part of the share which the Western churches must take in the whole world campaign, and while much can be done in the great centers where he is mainly to be found, it is on the quality of the life of the churches he has left behind that most depends.

Third, there is money. I have indicated in an earlier chapter how difficult are some of the problems that inhere in the use of foreign funds in the prosecution of Christian work in the East. It is only necessary to add that these questions are the subject of the most unremitting study on the part of those most intimately concerned. No one need have any doubt that every farthing given to a missionary society will be used with an economy and a fruitfulness that compare favorably with anything in our homelands. The generosity of the Christians of the East in relation to their resources, which are mostly very small, is literally astounding. I remember some years ago noticing in the published report of a Hindu public conference a speech by a leading Hindu who had gathered from some source or other figures of the giving of Indian Christians to their religious organizations. He was astonished. Says Mr. Phillips : " When one of the elders at the harvest thanksgiving gives a sheep or a calf, which is not uncommon, it means as much as if his opposite number in the West gave his motorcar, which *is* uncommon." [3] It is well to emphasize the

[3] *The Untouchables' Quest*, p. 58.

dangers which an unwise use of foreign money can bring with it to the indigenous churches, but when full allowance has been made for that, it remains abundantly true that the great tasks to which the whole church is called in the East require, if they are to be accomplished, the generosity of the older churches of the West with their enormously greater resources.

Perhaps it is worth saying here that we have all to get used to the church basis of work in the East, and not least in the matter of giving. I doubt whether those who give to missionary work as yet sense this need as fully as they ought. It is simple. to think in terms of "our mission in China," and I have shown that the missionary and his society are needed and will be needed for many a year yet. But it is essential that we should be prepared also to help and to give to the work conceived of as *the work of the church* and to foster in ourselves the same sort of personal and affectionate interest in the growing churches that is widely felt, thank God, toward the missions to which for so many years prayers and gifts have gone forth. We need much more of the sort of evidence which the Indian Mission of Fellowship to Great Britain and Ireland supplied, in its demonstration that there does actually exist a church of Jesus Christ in these far-off lands, different from our own congregations—and yet how much like them !

But now we come to what for the mass of us Christian people in the West is the root of the matter. There is no service that we can render to the churches in the East or in Africa greater than this : that our own witness be pure, brave, informed, humble and

united. To say this is not, indeed, to say—as some
unwisely do—that it is useless to aid missionary work
until our own church life is on a higher level. For
" we preach not ourselves, but Christ Jesus our
Lord." If Western Christianity were to be blotted
out there is a seed sown that will grow. But they
take a dangerous line who urge that Western Christianity and the life of the Western nations is in the
main a liability, and that the way forward is to separate the gospel from its Western historic setting. It
cannot be done, and it ought not to be tried. It is
right that non-Christian peoples should ask themselves what fruits the gospel has borne in the West.
Why should they expect it to do anything for them if
they are told by the earnest but misguided evangelist
that they must not worry their heads about what it
has done in the West ? But as I have said, the thing
is impossible. Such events as the betrayal of Abys-
sinia cannot be hid, and they are discussed, and their
bearing upon the quality of life of the Christian West
considered wherever intelligent people meet in the
East.

What would it not mean for the whole church of
Christ in the world, and not least in the Eastern
world, if there were a revival of deep and true religion in England or Scotland, in Germany or in
America ? I should rather say—What *does* it not
mean ? The echoes of the brave stand of the German
Confessional Synod and of the theological deepening
that has accompanied it have gone out into all the
world. The Group movement, in so far as it has
offered the hope of a new and spontaneous lay witness of wholehearted Christian discipleship, has at-

tracted attention literally everywhere. Men and women laboring in the obscure places in our own country, seeking to understand and obey the word of God as he speaks to them in their own place and time, are in vital and immediate touch, through the fellowship of the Holy Spirit, with all other Christians.

I have referred to the crying need for unity in the work of the church abroad. Need I say that that unity is withheld not only, nor in my judgment principally, by the divisive tendencies of the local Christians themselves—though they exist—but even more by the inability of the long separated Western churches to overcome their historic divisions? It is an open question whether it is going to be possible to get much further with plans for unity in the Eastern countries and in Africa unless the crucial questions are faced in the Western churches with the same keen desire to overcome them. There is tenfold more unity of action among the missionary societies than among the churches of which they are the instruments. Perhaps the gift that at this moment the younger churches can best give to the older is the realization that it is in the common fellowship of the evangelistic task that the lines of separation become not merely inconvenient but intolerable. If we were all keener to see our own country with its great unchurched masses won for Christ we should be in the temper which truly longs for unity.

There is the task of Christian thought. I have referred to the great forthcoming world meeting to be held at Oxford on the theme " Church, Community and State." It is being held with the purpose and in the hope that light may be shed on some of the central questions which confront Christians as they face the modern world. Manifestly these questions are world-wide—I trust that this book has made that plain, if it were doubted—and great benefits will come to the younger churches if the older, with their greater store of Christian training and intellectual equipment, can think and pray their way through to a clearer presentation of the word that God would have the church speak today.

It seems to me that one of the tasks most clearly laid upon our generation is to make real the ecumenical fellowship of the Christian church. Ideally this means a united church, and for that we pray and work. But there is much that can be done short of that longed-for consummation. Is it realized that today there is probably a more extensive personal friendship among men and women of all nations who bear burdens of leadership and service within the different churches than, probably, at any time in modern history? It is tempting—and there are many who yield to the temptation with singularly little resistance—to laugh easily at the rather numerous international Christian organizations and to write them off as talking shops, wasteful of the time of men who should be occupied with real things. The World Conference on Faith and Order ; the Universal Christian Council for Life and Work; the International Missionary Council ; the World's Student Christian Federation ; the World's Alliances of Young Men's and Young Women's Christian associations ; the World Alliance of the Churches for International Friendship—even these are by no means all, and most Christians have heard of none of them ! But taken together they do mean, as I have said, a personal friendship among Christians of all nations which to those who know it is unspeakably precious. But the times are instant upon us and we ought not to be content with this. It is, I believe, a peculiar task of our generation to give to this ecumenical Christian movement—for it is that and not merely an aggregation of different bodies—more of an outward reality and a greater vigor and decisiveness in action.

But I would not end on the note of human effort. Let us go back to the great certainties. I have more than once insisted on the connection between the prophetic religion of the Hebrews and the Christian revelation and the church which is rooted in it. The prophets looked forward to the day of the Lord. Jesus Christ did not so look forward. He announced that the kingdom had come. It was the belief of the first Christians that the consummation of all things to which the prophets looked forward with straining gaze had come to pass in the life, death, resurrection and ascension of the Lord. To that supreme act of the eternal God within the bounds of space and time the church has always looked in adoration, and found in it the anchor of its thought.

A preacher before the undergraduates of Oxford recently suggested that St. Paul, or one of his fellowship, would say, not as we do, " I wonder what the world is coming to," but " *I know what has come to the world.*" Christ Jesus has come, the Savior, full of grace and truth.

We are called not merely to hope, but to realize in our lives and in the communities of which we form a part that outpouring of the spirit and power of God for which the prophets looked in the day of the Lord, and which is called in St. John's Gospel the gift of eternal life. All that the Lord Jesus was in his life, all that he did for us in his dying upon the cross, all that wonderful release of power in Pentecost, these all are with us now, for us to make them our own. We do not know what lies before us, nor how hard the times may be. But we shall never be as those who only look to the future for deliverance, and expect in the future a golden age, for he has come, he is with us, and in him we can do all things.

" Lo I am with you always, even until the end of the world."

BOOKS FOR FURTHER READING

Asiatic Asia, S. K. Datta (Faber).

The Rural Mission of the Church in Eastern Asia, K. L. Butterfield (International Missionary Council).

Land and Labour in China, R. H. Tawney (Allen & Unwin).

Farm and Factory in China, J. B. Tayler (Student Christian Movement Press).

China Christian Year Book (obtainable from London Missionary Society).

The Chinese Church in Action, J. Foster (Edinburgh House Press).

Indian Industry, M. C. Matheson (Oxford University Press).

The Christian Mission in Rural India, K. Butterfield (International Missionary Council).

Socrates in an Indian Village, F. L. Brayne (Oxford University Press).

Behind Mud Walls, C. V. and W. H. Wiser (Allen & Unwin).

The Indian Peasant Uprooted, M. Read (Longmans).

Christ and Japan, T. Kagawa (Student Christian Movement Press).

Japan Christian Year Book (Kegan Paul).

Problem of the Far East, S. Mogi and H. V. Redman (Gollancz).

Christianity, Edwyn Bevan (Thornton Butterworth).

An Interpretation of Christian Ethics, Reinhold Niebuhr (Student Christian Movement Press).

The Apostolic Preaching and its Developments, C. H. Dodd (Hodder & Stoughton ; Willett, Clark).

A Faith for the World, W. Paton (Edinburgh House Press).

The Faiths of Mankind, W. Paton (Student Christian Movement Press).

Religion and the Modern State, Christopher Dawson (Sheed & Ward).

MAGAZINES

International Review of Missions. Published quarterly. Obtainable from Edinburgh House Press, 2 Eaton Gate, London, S.W.1.

National Christian Council of India Review. Published monthly. Obtainable from Edinburgh House Press.

The Chinese Recorder. Published monthly. Obtainable from 169 Yuen Ming Yuen Road, Shanghai, China.

The Moslem World. Published quarterly. Obtainable from Room 1023, 156 Fifth Avenue, New York.

Japan Christian Quarterly. Obtainable from Christian Literature Society of Japan, Kyo Bun Kwan, Ginza, Tokyo, Japan.

East and West Review. Published quarterly. Obtainable from S.P.C.K. House, Northumberland Avenue, London, W.C.

INDEX

UNION THEOLOGICAL SEMINARY
LIBRARY
NEW YORK